Needs-Based Market Segmentation Strategies:
How to Forecast Competitive Positions (and Make Millions)

James R. Taylor

Emeritus Professor of Marketing
Ross School of Business
University of Michigan

Cover design by Vila Design

Published by Van Rye Publishing, LLC
Ann Arbor, MI
www.vanryepublishing.com

ISBN: 978-1-7340344-8-6 (paperback)
ISBN: 978-1-7340344-9-3 (ebook)
Library of Congress Control Number: 2021949141

Praise for *Needs-Based Market Segmentation Strategies*

"An enjoyable read! Cleverly written as a refresher of lessons learned as an MBA student, this is an insightful discussion of needs-based market segmentation and its strategic significance in business success. A solid reminder to always understand the 'rules of the game' and listen to the 'voice of the customer!'"
—Fred Colony, Vice President and General Manager, HNI International, Muscatine, IA

"This latest book by Professor Taylor is everything one would expect from someone who has spent a career connecting market research and expertise to the development of successful market-based strategies in highly competitive markets. In this book, Dr. Taylor draws on his expertise working in industry, his career as a teacher-scholar, and his experience teaching business professionals across the globe. The lessons are particularly valuable for marketing practitioners and executives seeking to learn more."
—Michael D. Johnson, Ph.D., President, John Carroll University; Professor and Dean Emeritus, Cornell University School of Hotel Administration

"Professor Taylor has succinctly demonstrated the value of needs-based segmentation in executing a marketing and business strategy. The case studies presented in this book draw a direct linkage from the statistical analysis of a market need to the decision-making process required of business leadership in order to drive success within their respective businesses. Entrepreneurs, executive leadership, and business professionals can develop insights into how the concepts presented in this book can impact their business."

—Eric G. Williams, President and CEO, The Obscidion Group

"The writing style of this book is very easy to read, and the key messages resonated with me given my now seventeen years of marketing experience. I am a major advocate of needs-based segmentation. At Land O'Lakes, we follow a very similar methodology to what is described by Professor Taylor in this book. . . . I enjoyed how a wide range of needs-based research studies are discussed. . . . I especially got a kick out of reading the Campbell's Soup example, given my ten years at General Mills . . . and the many competitive battles between Progresso and Campbell's that came after the needs-based research. The Mobil Oil example also rang true, as we also find needs-based segmentation with commoditized businesses. I also liked the commentary on and payoff of how needs-based segmentation might just be the key to picking winning stocks. We all wish we had made the investments that Bob made, as described in this book, and could retire early!"

—James Kinnear, Marketing Director, Land O'Lakes Inc.

Dedication

Professor Clyde H. Coombs
1912–1988

Clyde was very influential in my career. He was a stellar
professor and an avid Michigan fan. Clyde was the founder of
the Mathematical Psychology Program at the University of
Michigan and retired as Emeritus Professor of Psychology.

Contents

Preface

THIS BOOK IS the result of requests from students and business executives to have a document that summarizes the material that Professor James Taylor presented in MBA classes and executive education programs during his over forty-year teaching and research career at the University of Michigan's famed Ross School of Business. Market segmentation is the division of potential customers into groups based on a wide range of characteristics (demographics, income and education levels, interests, etc.). This is now a booming industry of its own and is very much in the news with businesses' growing use of deep personal data to target groups or even individual customers. Needs-based segmentation, as presented in this book, is a new, innovative form of market segmentation that focuses on under-standing market dynamics and competitive performance.

How often have you heard someone say they would be a millionaire if only they had bought a glamour stock when it was first on the market? For example, if you bought shares of Amazon a decade ago, you're likely feeling good about your investment today. A $1,000 investment made in June 2011 would be worth $17,957.70, or a gain of 1,695.77%, as of June 11, 2021.

Why is it so easy to have great hindsight about Amazon today and so difficult to have great foresight about Amazon ten years ago? The answer is that hindsight is based on widely communicated historical facts, whereas foresight is typically based on speculation and weak information regarding a firm's future competitive position in a market. The key lesson is that current and future needs of the marketplace—both consumer needs and business needs—are what determine a firm's success or failure. The firm's success or failure is *not* determined just by seemingly impressive characteristics of the firm.

The problem for investors is that accurate facts regarding the needs of a market are not widely understood, and obtaining those facts requires investors to utilize market research processes to obtain accurate data. The secret insight for investors is that marketplace needs are stable and change slowly as businesses move into the future. So, measuring today's market needs allows accurate forecasts of future consumer and business needs and competitive performance.

This book's central theme is that research processes such as needs-based market segmentation can provide market-based facts that forecast the future success and failure of competitors in a market over time. The book's target audience is business executives, investors, students, and educators who want a book that explains the needs-based segmentation process and presents real examples of successful executions of that process as a tool for strategic decision-making. The critical role of the needs-based segmentation process in addressing the strategic problems of leading business organizations is explained in detail along with real-world examples of businesses that have implemented policies based on needs-based segmentation intelligence. And, as described toward the end of this book, investors who learn to follow the process could even make millions!

Chapter 1

Strategic Marketing Class: Introduction to Basic Marketing Concepts

IN THIS CHAPTER, we will accompany a typical business school class as the students discover and explore fundamental concepts of marketing and economics and learn how to examine certain commonly believed ideas about stock picking and forecasting future markets. The students will go on to apply what they have learned to an in-depth study of the strategic marketing choices made by Southwest Airlines and by Kellogg's and Nestlé and to be introduced to the importance of market segmentation in those choices.

SETTING THE SCENE

It was hard for me to believe that it was the fall of 1984. The leaves were starting to signal the end of summer, and Ann Arbor was bustling with the beginning of a new school year. I strolled through the center of campus and headed to the University of Michigan's law school. The old gothic buildings were magnifi-

1

cent. The courtyard was filled with law students conversing and studying in the afternoon sun. Classes at the law school had begun a week earlier than those at the Ross School of Business.

Crossing the street, I arrived at the business school. Upon entering the main building, I passed by the registration table, where new students were picking up enrollment materials and name badges. The first year of the MBA program was a preset schedule of classes. I would be instructing two of the sections of a core Strategic Marketing class. Additional classes during the first-year MBA program included Accounting, Economics, Finance, and Quantitative Methods.

Classes did not start until after Labor Day. The weekend began with a football game in the famed Michigan Big House. My wife, Linda, and I had tickets with a group of faculty members. We always enjoyed the first game as signaling the start of a new academic year and as a chance to see old friends. Michigan played Colorado, and the game was rather lopsided, with Michigan winning 27-3. The giant stadium was always exciting, with a capacity of 100,474. After the game, we all had drinks and dinner at one of the faculty members' homes. The rest of my weekend was devoted to organizing for class.

The first day of classes involved the usual routine of seat assignments, syllabi, and imparting the instructor's expectations of students. My classes emphasized the use of the case method of teaching, which involved the Socratic method. This approach uses a dialogue between teacher and students, instigated by the continual probing questions of the teacher, in a concerted effort to explore the underlying beliefs that shape the students' views and opinions. It is a participatory, discussion-based way of learning, where students gain skills in critical thinking, communication, and group dynamics. My students typically found case studies to be a refreshing way to learn and enjoyed the dynamic classroom environment.

Our first few sessions, replicated in part in the following sections of this chapter, would lay the groundwork for the rigorous thinking I expected from my students. We would look at basic concepts and do a "reality check" on our ability to forecast future events and to forecast stock market prices ("stock picking").

Figure 1.1. Exterior View of the University of Michigan's Ross School of Business

FORECASTING FUTURE EVENTS

Developing realistic future business scenarios is central to the success of a business's strategic planning process. The case study students used to explore this issue was based on the so-called Hubbert model of energy production. In March 1956, M. King Hubbert, a research scientist for Shell Oil, predicted that oil production from forty-eight contiguous states in the United States would peak between 1965 and 1970. Hubbert's predictions were initially called by many "utterly ridiculous." But when US oil production peaked in 1970, he became an instant celebrity and a living legend.

Hubbert based his estimate on a mathematical model that assumes the production of a resource follows a bell-shaped curve—one that rises rapidly to a peak and declines just as quickly. After the peak of the early 1970s, actual US oil production declined, consistent with Hubbert's prediction up to the then-current date of 1986.

The class assignment was to analyze the Hubbert model and defend or reject his forecast of a decline in oil production through 2010. The case study included the complete report by Hubbert, which involved many pages of charts and statistics. After reading through the case study, the students' reaction was often "Why me?" However, they were required to take a position and find sound reasons for support. Students formed study group teams and would meet after class to discuss the case.

The next class began with a show of hands of those who supported Hubbert's predictions and then those who opposed. The safe position was to support the predictions, but a few brave souls raised their hands in opposition. The next hour involved an intense debate about the assumptions in the model and why they could be in error. At the end of the discussion, I summarized key student themes.

The first theme was the role of technology and the difficulty in forecasting future innovations in oil extraction. Of course, today, we know that innovations in fracking technology have substantially increased the amount of oil extracted. Second, estimates of world oil reserves of 600 billion barrels by 2010 could be challenged. By 1995, the US Geological Survey raised this estimate of the amount of oil in the ground to 3 trillion barrels. Third, the role of substitutes must be considered. At the time, the high cost of wind, solar, and natural gas limited student arguments that they would replace oil. But today, the cost of natural gas has significantly dropped due to fracking innovations. The lesson for the class was that forecasting the future is difficult and that underlying assumptions must be understood and rigorously challenged.

The Hubbert model case study expanded students' perspectives on the difficulty of forecasting the future business environment. The focus now turned to forecasting future stock prices. Buying stocks low and selling them high seemed to be a great way to get rich. Students were excited to explore this issue.

PICKING STOCKS

I started the class by making the statement that stock picking is almost always a losing game. You could see the surprise on students' faces. So, why is it such a failing activity? The prices of stocks are constantly adjusting to the news that is available to the public. Without insider information, it's very difficult to forecast future events of a company. Unfortunately, trading stocks based on insider information is illegal. I smiled and said that if accurate stock picking were possible, I would be enjoying living on a half-million-dollar yacht rather than leading the life of a poor college professor.

The class was then invited to open a discussion to challenge my position. Students were eager to participate in a heated discussion. It started with a student asking, "If stock picking is so hopelessly futile, why does the media continue to focus on it? Why do brokers continue selling it? Why do individual investors keep buying stocks? Why are TV programs and newsletters devoted to giving stock picks? Why are 'stock guru' recommendations and predictions so prevalent?"

After patiently listening to the class but not giving clear answers, I assigned study teams to report the results of research studies addressing the questions raised in class. Each study group was to summarize the findings of a research report and, if appropriate, challenge the findings. For example, one group was assigned a report by two finance professors titled "The Stock Performance of Individual Investors." The report reviewed and summarized the vast amount of research on the stock trading behavior of individual investors. The group reported the following key findings of the study to the class:

- Individual investors underperform low-cost index funds, which are the standard benchmark.
- Individual investors exhibit the "disposition effect": selling winning investments while holding on to losing investments.
- Individual investors exhibit "naïve reinforcement learning" by repeating positive past behavior while avoiding painful past experiences.
- Individual investors tend to maintain undiversified stock portfolios.

The next two classes were devoted to students' reports on the research studies. What did we take away from all this overload of information? The main message is that individual stock trading can be very dangerous to one's wealth. Overconfidence explains the existing high levels of stock trading and the poor performance of individual investors. When the average individual decides to trade in stocks, they are competing against an army of Ph.D. quant jocks hired by Warren Buffett, who spend hours analyzing data. Why does the individual investor think they have more information than these professionals? For many students, the dream of making millions by stock trading was now in question.

I ended the question about forecasting stock prices with a story about the physicist Isaac Newton. By the spring of 1720, Newton was one of the most famous scientists in the world and was a very wealthy man. He decided to speculate on London's South Sea bubble and later sold his shares in the South Sea Co., earning $2 million in today's money. He was said to be worried the market was getting out of hand, and he supposedly quipped that he "can calculate the motions of heavenly bodies but not the madness of the people." A few months later, the stock market moved higher, and he let his own madness get the best of him. Newton got back in and lost the equivalent of $3.6 million in today's dollars when the market crashed.

DIGGING INTO MARKET STRATEGY AND COMPETITIVE ADVANTAGE: SOUTHWEST AIRLINES CASE STUDY

The class then delved into the key concepts underlying market strategies and competitive advantage. We uncovered the concepts of obvious costs vs. hidden and opportunity costs through several case studies. Our first case study looked at Southwest Airlines, where we saw how obvious benefits, such as newer technology or a wider range of service, can mask several hidden costs. The choice of simplicity can allow significant cost reduction, while a focus on hiring team players and on employee well-being can generate superior service. We then looked at an unsuccessful attempt by Kellogg's to penetrate the Indian breakfast foods market, compared to a more successful one by Nestle—which did better research on the needs of the Indian market—and some further examples of effective consultation of consumers.

I started the class by probing students on an array of issues.

What is strategy? Why are some industries more attractive than others? Is money a source of competitive advantage? What are the drivers of competitive advantage? Why is market growth important? Why do some businesses succeed and others fail? Does business create demand for products and services? Class time went by in a flash. Students found it exciting to participate in a lively debate on issues they had never thought about in detail. I ended the class by indicating that the next several weeks would be devoted to analyzing these and other marketing strategy issues. (For a definition of "Marketing Strategy," see Appendix C: Terminology Used in This Book.)

The next case study assignment was about Southwest Airlines (SWA).[1] I indicated that SWA was an example of a very successful and profitable company in an unattractive industry, evolving from regulation to deregulation. The assignment was to explain SWA's drivers of success and evaluate SWA's future courses of action.

The case study discussed the airline's founding in 1967, which was delayed for four years due to court battles brought by competitors who contested the carrier's entrance into the Texas intrastate market. All Southwest flights out of Dallas originated from Love Field, where the corporate offices of Southwest were located. The marketing department developed a positioning strategy described as "obviously fun," to differentiate the airline from its competition. The positioning strategy revolved around "Love Potions"—an on-board drink—and a "Love Machine" that instantly dispensed plane tickets. The advertising message was, "There is somebody else up there who loves you."

Southwest offered low, unrestricted fares and eight or more on-time, one-way flights a day on specific routes. The initial routes involved the love triangle, which was Dallas to San Antonio and return, San Antonio to Houston and return, and Houston to Dallas and return. The love triangle enabled business and leisure travelers who might have otherwise driven the distance between the three cities to fly instead.

Southwest grew steadily during the 1970s. However, the airline faced the challenge of deregulation as well as pressures for growth by market expansion. Critics argued that changes to SWA policies of no meals, no preassigned seats, and no membership in an airline reservation system were critical to future success, as was the transition to a hub and spoke route system.

The next two class sessions were devoted to heated debates about Southwest's advantages and disadvantages, why it had been successful, and what actions it should take in the future. I presented challenging insights to the student positions taken. The closing assignment was for each study group to prepare a summary paper discussing the key lessons to be learned from the classroom discussions. Each team was to present a short overview of its paper to the class and to provide each study group a copy of its main paper.

Students spent the weekend reading the study group papers in search of the key insights to the question of how successful organizations make big bucks. Here are the main points reported. First, a business model that focuses on target markets can have a clear competitive advantage over an unfocused business. Second, strategy is about choices, and choices involve understanding the trade-offs between benefits offered and the organizational costs of those benefits. Third, the customer is the only judge of the Benefit/Price value proposition offered by a business.

We considered the target markets for SWA. There were two segments of buyers: business travelers and leisure travelers. They represent the classic example of the strategic challenge in designing a positioning strategy for two different segments. Leisure travelers are more price-sensitive than business passengers since they must pay for the travel out of pocket. For short hauls, the price sensitivity is determined by the cost and convenience of driving a car. While the option of charging a higher price to target the business segment seems attractive, it also limits access to the larger and growing leisure segment. SWA made the strategic choice of volume vs. margin to remain attractive to the price-sensitive leisure segment, which had the potential to grow.

The choice of lower price turned the strategic discussion into one of costs. Airlines have three main cost centers: planes, fuel, and employees. Planes and fuel offer limited opportunity to gain a sustainable competitive advantage due to their commodity nature. Consequently, SWA developed a competitive advantage through the design of a focused/simplified business model and superior employee management practices.

SWA Business Model

I started the class by asking why SWA only purchased standard Boeing 737s. Wouldn't it be better to buy different planes that better fit the needs of different routes and customer groups? The discussion focused on the strategy of simplicity. Keeping it simple, with one plane, allows lower costs in the areas of spare parts, pilot training, and mechanic training. I emphasized that in most companies, the manager's job is to manage complexity.

Consider an engineer who must buy a new drill system. Is the best drill one that has the latest new technology, or is it the older, lower-cost model which would lower organizational costs? The key learning point was that the trade-off between benefits and costs is rarely considered since the advantages of new benefits are easy to see while the cost of complexity is hidden by the accounting system.

The discussion of hidden costs was highlighted with a story

about a man who loses his car keys at night, near his car. A passerby stops to help and asks, "Where did you drop the keys?" The man says, "Near the trunk." Passerby says, "So, why are you looking at the front of the car?" Man says, "The light is better here." The learning point is that companies look where the light is good. Benefits are easy to see, and the costs of delivering the benefits are often hidden in the dark of the accounting system.

Consider SWA's decision to not offer meals. When one checks the income statements of a SWA competitor, you find that meals cost $7.70 per person. Market research shows that customers are willing to pay $10.00 for a hot meal. That is a $2.30 profit. But SWA says this is the wrong way to look at things. Instead, where did the costs of adding a food galley go? How about the opportunity cost of losing two rows of seats? One must also add an additional flight attendant to prepare and serve the food. How about the loss of turnaround time due to cleanup and loading food on board? Remember, one now needs a VP of Food Management back at headquarters.

So, how does the accounting system treat the real costs? It does so by allocating most costs to other areas. Consequently, many of the real costs become hidden. The hidden and opportunity costs are not considered in an accounting system. When this issue was raised in my accounting class, it became clear that accounting is more about following accounting rules than about identifying information for strategic decision-making.

An interesting SWA strategic decision involves not having assigned seats. The savings here are: no software system for seat assignment, no ticket agent involved, and faster turn time for the planes. What drives faster turn time? In the SWA system, the boarding process is faster since passengers queue at the gate to be first for a good seat. Clearly, opportunity costs and hidden costs are very important strategic issues in understanding competitive advantage. The message to be learned was that the "total strategic costs" involve obvious costs, hidden costs, and opportunity costs.

The last area of competitive advantage relates to the organizational culture of management and employees. SWA employees state that SWA is a fun place to work. They are loyal, energetic, flexible, empowered, proud, take ownership, and are team/family oriented. Management style involves direct/personal contact with employees. There is friendly, accessible, and free-flowing family-style communication.

I asked the class how SWA can so uniquely hire this type of employee when all companies want them. The answer is a recruiting process based on attitude selection vs. qualifications. What is needed to implement a recruiting process like this in a company? The answer is a large selection/training budget, if hiring based on attitude is required.

It is easy and cheap to narrow 200 resumes down to 20 based on skills identified on a resume. This is not possible when screening on attitude, though. Ask people if they are team-oriented, and they will, of course, say yes. Instead, SWA has a daylong interview process that involves groups of candidates participating in activities, much like a party environment. SWA believes they need to see potential employees in the group environment to know that they have the proper attitude and team capabilities. Was this possibly a key dimension to a sustainable competitive advantage?

Class Assignment

I summarized the class discussion of SWA by presenting a diagram called the "Value/Cost Delivery Model" (or "Value/Cost Matrix"), as shown in Figure 1.2 that follows. This model is used to identify the drivers of "Value Differentiation" and "Cost Differentiation" as explained in the related Class Teaching Note that I distributed to the class (see Appendix A: Class Note—Strategic Concepts and Processes in Business Strategy). The "Value/Cost Matrix" evaluates the strategic positioning of competitors in a target segment of a market.

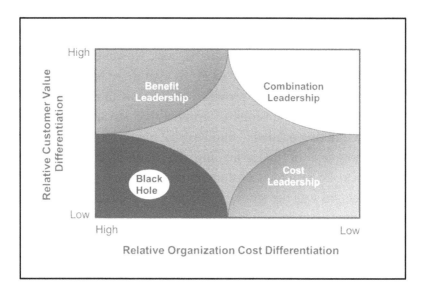

Figure 1.2. Value/Cost Matrix

The class assignment was to review the Class Teaching Note (at Appendix A) and evaluate the conclusion that SWA is in a Combination Leadership position in the leisure segment of the value/cost matrix. What is SWA's competitive position in the business segment? What is the competitive position of United Airlines in the leisure segment and the business segment? What changes should be made to the SWA strategy, if any?

I ended the class by emphasizing that growth is important to a business for several reasons. If the firm can grow faster than competitors, its stock will rise, and shareholders will be happy. In addition, employee morale goes up when the team is winning. This is especially the case for SWA since all employees receive stock as part of the employment package. Additionally, SWA's low-price strategy started to grow the number of leisure travelers in the US as a result of its competitors' response with even lower fares. I reminded the class of a story: one SWA customer said the low prices were both good and bad. He explained, "I can now travel with my family at a reasonable cost. However, cheap fares mean that my mother-in-law wants to visit more often."

The SWA case study provided students with a clear under-standing of the dimensions of competitive advantage and the strategic thinking needed to build a great organization. First came the importance of understanding the trade-offs between the benefits to be provided customers and the true organizational costs. Second was the strategic choice of a focus on target mar-kets vs. the attraction of a multi-market strategy that seeks greater revenue. Third was the attraction of a low-price strategy and its relationship to lower organizational costs through simplicity. However, I emphasized that a successful strategy rarely has unlimited sustainability. The challenge for SWA was how to maintain an advantage and grow the business.

SWA Strategic Choices

The class discussion turned to a heated debate over SWA's future strategic choices. One camp advocated for no strategic changes, other than expanding to new cities that had the characteristics of the "love triangle" cities. The focus was on high-traffic markets like Boston to NYC to Washington DC. Others argued for chang-es in the Value/Cost Delivery Model, such as meals, assigned seats, longer flights, etc. The impact of such changes on the leisure and business segments were heatedly debated. The underlying strategy challenge was how to grow the business and maintain a competitive advantage.

Dissecting the SWA case study challenged the students' understanding of the complexity and discipline required in designing a successful business model with a sustainable competitive advantage. Becoming a successful entrepreneur seemed rather challenging and highly uncertain for many students. Was the SWA start-up management just lucky to be in Dallas at the time when an opportunity for a new business model had presented itself? Clearly, the founders became very rich as a result of the rising stock price. How does one figure out where to look for the next SWA-type opportunity? How can one be at the right place at the right time, with the resources to build a great company?

In the SWA case study, recognizing the needs of the two market segments was key in designing the business model. The business segment was smaller in size than the leisure segment but less price sensitive. The leisure segment was larger and growing but required a lower price, competitive with driving a car. Targeting the leisure segment required a business model that focused on a lower cost structure while providing the key benefits of a convenient schedule, speed, and selective service.

The SWA case study demonstrated that designing an innovative business model based on solid marketing strategy and business principles can lead to great success. The founders of SWA became very rich people. SWA's founders appeared to be bright individuals who were in the right place at the right time and were willing to take risks and devote years of hard work to build a very successful business. Being part of the airline business in the Dallas market gave them practical experience regarding the market for air travel. They clearly had a vision of the opportunity for a low-cost airline and took a gamble. A lot can be learned from the SWA experience, including that riches come from solid strategic choices and years of hard work.

Results of SWA's Strategic Choices

SWA pursued a conservative growth strategy that focused on the leisure market segment in short-haul markets throughout the US. Expansion within the then-current route structure was the priority. As customer volume increased, Southwest used new planes to add capacity to the current system or to add nonstop flights between cities previously connected by one-stop service. Eighty-five percent of SWA expansion was from internal growth. The following figure is a flowchart showing SWA's Value/Cost Delivery Model.

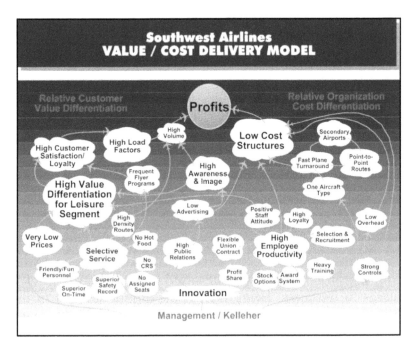

Figure 1.3. Southwest Airlines Value/Cost Delivery Model

16

In addition, SWA slowly expanded to western, northern, and eastern cities. This external expansion was often opportunity-driven. For example, with the collapse of Midway Airlines in 1991, SWA had the opportunity to move into Midway Airport in Chicago and establish an anchor in the Midwest. A low pricing strategy was always maintained.

Dave Ridley, director of marketing, stated, "We do it by pricing against ground transportation as much as against exiting air service. This results in prices at least 60% below competitive airfares and sometimes 75% or 80% below. Of course, we must be able to sustain and make money at these prices, which we can do because of our low operating cost."[2] SWA maintained this focused strategy over the years and experienced substantial growth in profits and stock price, as shown in the following figure.

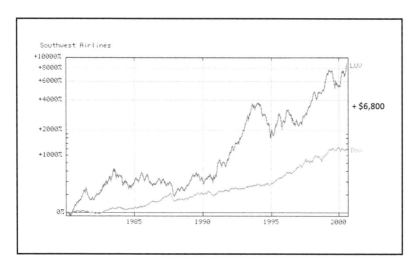

Figure 1.4. Stock Chart: Southwest Airlines shareholder Wealth Versus the Dow Average (to 2000)

KEY LESSON LEARNED ABOUT STRATEGIC CHOICES

What is strategy about? In one word, strategy is about *choice*: making choices to win. If you simply copy the competition, you will lose. If there are only two competitors in the market, you end up in a draw—no one wins. Einstein defined insanity as doing the same thing again and expecting different results. Managers must make controversial choices to win. Most companies reduce strategy to a trivial statement: "High-quality products sold at a low price." This is not a statement of strategy. And the opposite is not a choice: "Low-quality products sold at a high price." Strategy is a real choice, and it is by nature controversial. If it is not controversial, it is not interesting from a strategy perspective.

Strategic choices are controversial because good arguments are present on both sides of the choice. If there is no opposite side, the choice is not strategic. Good analysis requires the clear presentation of both sides of the choice. This reflects the debate and risk inherent in strategic choice. Mathematics is not controversial. Consequently, there is no strategy in mathematics. There is a right and wrong answer that can be proven with principles and laws.

To have a competitive, differential advantage in the future, wise choices must be made today. Choices must be made about which market segments to compete in and how to compete in those segments. Market segments require quantitative information about what is important to the customer segment and how to gain a sustainable competitive advantage. Singapore Airlines was the first to innovate with a hot towel for customers. Did this give them a sustainable competitive advantage? No, it is too easy to copy. How fast can it be copied? One month? This is not strategy because strategy is defined as long run, not a month. Strategy should be for at least three years, or longer-term.

Consider the following story about competitive advantage. Two campers are in the Canadian North woods. During the night, one camper is awakened by the sound of a grizzly bear approaching the campsite. He jumps up, warning his friend, and starts to run into the woods. Looking back in surprise, he can see his friend stopping to put on his Nike running shoes. He calls back, "Hurry, don't you know that a grizzly can outrun a man?" The friend says, "Yes, but I only have to outrun you." Strategy is the counterpart to the shoes. Strategic choice is about finding the shoes.

KELLOGG'S CORN FLAKES VS. NESTLE

The next case study in the Marketing Strategy class expanded the focus on understanding segment needs and the positioning of benefits to needs.[3] The case study was about Kellogg's entry into the Indian market with Kellogg's US-leading brand of cereal called Corn Flakes. Kellogg's strategic objective was to achieve growth with entry into the expanding Indian market.

Kellogg's target market in India was the rich, urbanized, Westernized part of the population. The company quickly achieved reasonable success, building on its superior product quality and brand equity. However, two years later, sales started to decline. In response, Kellogg decided to lower its price and expand the target market to more traditional upper-class Indian customers. The new marketing program was a failure.

My students were assigned to explore what went wrong. Before the discussion began, I set a restriction that students from India could not enter the discussion. The remainder of the class speculated about potential problems such as product quality issues, competitors price-cutting, and weak advertising/promotion.

I then invited five Indian students to come down in front of the class for a focus-group-style interview. The discussion turned to what breakfast was like as they grew up in India. The five students were from the upper class in India and were representative of Kellogg's target market. The students explained that they typically ate a hot breakfast and would put heated milk on their cereal. Using cold milk on cereal is culturally alien to them. The Indian students also pointed out that Corn Flakes is an expensive breakfast.

Kellogg's value proposition of a crunchy cereal, which was successful in the US, was not carrying over to India as it discovered that the hot milk resulted in a soggy cereal. The local competitor of corn flakes is formulated to stay crunchy in hot milk and sells at a lower price. Why would the Indian consumer pay a higher price for soggy cereal? The message students came away with was that a successful marketing strategy must fit the needs of the market better than that of the competition. The important insight is that market needs can be uncovered by listening to the customer.

A key competitor, Nestlé, took a very different strategic approach in the Indian market. It seized the Indian opportunity by creating a whole range of reasonably-priced products that can be used to quickly prepare a traditional Indian breakfast. By combining its skills in food processing, marketing, packaging, and distribution with an understanding of the local market, Nestlé expanded the breakfast segment of the market. The Nestlé story reinforced the main lesson of the day: understanding market needs and positioning the marketing program to those needs is key to gaining a sustainable competitive advantage.

The next marketing class was devoted to summarizing many of the lessons that had been learned. In emerging markets, it is important to understand the trap of hidden purchasing power. For example, in India, 40% of people's purchasing power is from income not reported. As marketers, what does this mean? This hidden purchasing power drives the demand of expensive products and fashion items since buyers cannot put the money in a bank for fear it would show as unreported income. Of course, this high purchasing power segment is very attractive to importers from advanced economies. This segment is most like that in advanced economies, and existing products can be marketed without major modification.

The strategic trap is that market needs and the requirements of the home market rarely are the same in the emerging market. This is the lesson from the Kellogg case study. I contrasted the Kellogg situation with that of Unilever selling shampoo in Indonesia.

Unilever discovered that most Indonesians only use shampoo for a date or other special occasion since they can't afford to stock a full-sized bottle of shampoo. In response, Unilever developed a small package of shampoo to meet the needs of the customer. The result was a great success. Again, the lesson learned is that marketers must design the proper benefit/price mix to fit the requirement of the target market.

STRATEGIC PLANNING PROCESS

The remainder of the Marketing Strategy course was devoted to exploring the strategic planning process. (See Appendix A: Class Note—Strategic Concepts and Processes in Business Strategy, mentioned previously.) Case studies focused on evaluating the strategic plans of various firms. In addition, student teams were required to interview a local business and to evaluate the status of its strategic planning process.

This assignment was a real eye-opener for the class. The

evaluations typically highlighted the limited information that strategic plans had regarding market segments and the needs of customers in those segments. And most interviews indicated that this information was based on personal beliefs of managers and salespeople as to how customers buy their products.

I summarized this component of the class with the following list of points regarding the current state of marketing practice and what I foresaw as the future of successful marketing organizations.

Current Marketing Practice:

- Intuition- or experience-based decision-making in the strategic planning process.
- Lack of cost/price/profit understanding.
- Focus on brand monitoring and customer satisfaction reporting.
- Poor coordination among marketing, sales, and service.
- Marketing staffed by those with limited marketing training.

Future Marketing Practice:

- Fact-based information supporting all decisions with a cost/price/profit focus.
- Needs-based segmentation studies used for planning, targeting, and value proposition development.
- A rigorous strategy and tactical planning process.
- Marketing personnel that are formally trained.

With these points in mind, I encouraged students to consider taking my course on Market Research Procedures the following semester. I indicated that there are statistical methods designed to measure customer needs and quantify market segments. Such fact-based information could be the key to gaining a sustainable competitive advantage.

Chapter 2

Summer Consulting Adventure: OdorChem

THIS CHAPTER WILL show how gaining perspective on the needs of the buyer can lead a company to a very different strategy than the classic strategy of cutting prices when faced with a competitive threat. An Ann Arbor company offered an invaluable learning laboratory for a student intern, who learned how companies often focus on internal technical and financial numbers but remain unaware of the other forces that drive consumer choices.

Over the years, several local businesses had developed a strong relationship with the University of Michigan's Ross School of Business. Such was the case with the Arbor Corporation.[1] Each year, it offered to have a first-year MBA student work for the company over the summer months. I recommended a very bright student from my Marketing Strategy class by the name of Robert ("Bob") Swanson. Bob had a chemical engineering degree from Wisconsin and was a good fit for the Arbor Corporation.

The Arbor Corporation was a leader in RV components and supplies such as toilets, toilet chemicals, and other RV items. It was started in 1963 with an innovative "first slide-action valve for RV holding tanks." Later innovation included the first low-water-use RV toilet, low vacuum breaker toilet, and water seal RV toilet. The excellent management and technical staff included mechanical and chemical engineers, many with MBAs. A very important product was called OdorChem. It was the #1-selling holding tank deodorant in the US as well as a worldwide leader.

ODORCHEM THREAT

Bob's first assignment at Arbor Corporation involved assessing the competitive threat to OdorChem from a leading chemical giant. A major distributor, Camping World, notified Arbor Corporation's Sales Manager that a leading chemical company would be conducting a test market for a competitive product to Odor-Chem. Two weeks later, a case of the competitive product arrived at Arbor Corporation for evaluation. The chemical tests indicated that the competitive product was almost identical to the Odor-Chem formulation.

At a strategy meeting of management and chemists, the technical results of the tests were evaluated. The technical staff argued that the competitive product presented a serious threat to OdorChem. OdorChem controlled 70% of the market and was priced at a premium over current competition. Tests of the current competition indicated they were inferior products with formulations using cheaper chemicals.

The evolving strategic scenario was that a price cut was in order to protect market share and counter the competitive threat. However, the VP of Finance argued this would be a costly strategy and have a very negative impact on profits. At this point, the CEO suggested that I should be contacted for advice. Over the years, I had worked on several consulting projects with the Arbor

Corporation and had developed a strong personal relationship with it.

STRATEGY MEETING

My meeting with Arbor Corporation began at 9 a.m. in its main conference room. All participants from the previous meeting were available, and the technical staff presented the data on the new competitive product. The strategic concerns from the previous meeting were discussed in detail. I listened intently and asked several questions.

The first question was whether the customer benefits of OdorChem were primarily driven by the chemistry of the product. For the chemists in the meeting, the answer was clearly YES. After a lengthy debate, I recommended that a series of focus groups be conducted with customers of both OdorChem and its current competitors, to explore their reasons for purchasing the products. The recommendation was accepted by management, and a market research firm in Detroit was contacted to conduct the focus group sessions. Bob was put in charge of administering the project.

FOCUS GROUP RESULTS

Focus groups were conducted in three locations: Detroit, Boston, and Phoenix. The sessions were videotaped, and the market research firm transcribed the discussions and prepared a report on the results. Bob and I attended the session in Detroit. We sat behind a one-way glass window and had a chance to gain a clear perspective on how the buyers of RV toilet chemicals viewed the purchase process. Bob was very surprised at the difference between the technical staff's perspective of what was important in purchasing OdorChem (chemical formulation) and what the buyers said.

The focus group report supported my concerns. The primary benefits sought in the purchase of toilet chemicals were odor control and waste digestion. The price or cost of the products was important only for a few individuals. The interesting insight was the reaction of buyers to purchasing a new product instead of their regular brand. A typical response was, "Why would I take a chance on another brand when I know my brand works great?" It was clear that most buyers did not view a lower-priced competitor as a reason to take a chance on a potentially poor outcome. Clearly, having a clogged toilet or an invasive odor in the RV was not acceptable.

The formal focus group report was presented to Arbor Corporation at a meeting in Ann Arbor. Before the focus group results were presented, I emphasized that focus groups are just the first step in starting to understand the world of the buyer. They are based on small customer groups selected by convenience rather than on probability sample selection procedures. Ideas can be gained, which need to be supported by formal market research procedures.

The focus group findings suggest that the buyers of Odor-Chem perceived risk in trying a competitive product. A lower price was not an incentive to offset this significant risk. The recommendation was to conduct a scientific survey of OdorChem buyers and competitors to quantify the focus group findings. A sound strategic reaction to the competitive threat would require better market data, given the potential impact on profits of a price cut strategy. The management group discussed the research findings and considered my recommendation. After considerable debate, the second research project was approved. Again, Bob was to work with me on the second study.

NEEDS-BASED SEGMENTATION PROCEDURE AND RESULTS

Bob met with me at my office to plan the new study. A doctoral student named Rajah was assigned to design and manage the research project. The market research firm in Detroit would implement the fieldwork and tabulate the survey research data. Rajah was an expert in statistical analysis and would analyze the data using a procedure called Cluster Analysis.

The research study involved telephone interviews with Odor-Chem users and with users of competitive products. Two hundred and fifty interviews were conducted with buyers across the United States. Buyers were selected using probability sampling procedures.

One afternoon, Bob stopped by my office with an update on the research project. After the update, I asked him how the internship was going. He said the internship was a great opportunity to see the lessons learned in the Marketing Strategy class put into practice. It was exciting to realize that a small firm in Ann Arbor could quantify the US market for one of its products using market research techniques. He was eager to see the research findings and the reaction of Arbor Corporation's management.

The data tapes arrived from the market research firm, and Bob took them over to Rajah for analysis. Rajah indicated that the analysis and report would be completed in a week. Bob scheduled everyone for a meeting at Arbor Corporation two weeks out. This gave me time to review the results and prepare my recommendation.

RESEARCH FINDINGS

The meeting started at 9 a.m. in the board room of Arbor Corporation. Rajah and I gave an extensive presentation on the market for OdorChem and its competitors. Information on market size, usage patterns and rates, customer profiles by brand, regional differences, purchases by retail outlet, etc. were reviewed. What caught management's attention were the results of the cluster analysis, which identified the market segments.

Three market segments or clusters were presented. The largest segment (52%) preferred the product benefits of odor and waste control. The second segment (36%) preferred environment/safety first and odor/waste control second. The third segment (12%) preferred cost or lowest price over the other benefits.

My primary recommendation to Arbor Corporation was to not lower the price of OdorChem in response to the competitive threat. Instead, the product benefits of odor and waste control should be prominently displayed on the label and merchandising material. It was pointed out that the current label failed to do this by giving major space to the company name and product ingredients. A major packaging redesign was recommended. My second recommendation was to take advantage of the buyer's perceived risk in trying a new product. This could take the form of merchandising material such as shelf displays that communicate OdorChem's dominant market position.

My last recommendation involved new product line additions. The environment/safety segment represented an unmet need. This gap was a potential opportunity for competitive entry. The recommendation was to develop a new "green" OdorChem for this segment. The segment size was too big to ignore.

The final product line recommendation was for Arbor Corporation to consider a secondary brand that was lower priced. While this segment was small and did not represent an important profit opportunity, it would block price-cutting competitors. The downside was that retailers could display "Made by Arbor Corporation" next to the new product. This could cannibalize OdorChem sales.

After extensive discussion, Arbor Corporation accepted the recommendations, except for the development of a low-price product. Bob told me that he left the meeting with a new appreciation of the role of market research and segmentation in the strategic process. In a short period of time—two months—Arbor Corporation's management had addressed a serious competitive threat by using market-driven research tools that quantified the structure of the OdorChem market. The management group was willing to "listen" to the voice of the market and react with a new strategy. This was a wonderful learning experience for Bob. OdorChem was a live case study that he would never forget.

COMING TO AN END

The summer was ending, and I decided to invite Bob to lunch and explore his internship experience. He stated that he was most impressed with how hard it is for management to maintain a clear focus on the strategic realities of the marketplace. Daily operations drive the focus of management to internal organizational issues. Financial issues, supplier conflicts, personnel problems, and manufacturing problems pervade the daily activities for management.

When it comes to real numbers, readily available financial numbers dominate management's attention and decision-making. There are few numbers that represent the marketplace, other than financial revenue and reports from the sales force. The accounting system is filled with numbers that relate to costs.

Bob pointed to the first year of the MBA program, which is all about understanding accounting numbers and financial procedures and learning to analyze accounting ratios, money market issues, and the bottom line. Managers are trained to live in a bubble of internal data and personal observation. Every so often, management gets a peek at the real market numbers through studies like that done for OdorChem. Numbers representing the "voice of the customer" are not a routine part of daily operations. It is only when a competitive threat appears on the scene that smart management like that of Arbor Corporation calls upon outside consulting for advice.

Bob concluded his observations by stating how interested he was in the fall class on Market Research Procedures. It was clear that the summer internship had provided Bob with practical experience in understanding the importance of identifying market segments and implementing a business strategy. He was convinced that quantifying the structure of markets using market segmentation processes was essential to strategy development. I was pleased that the summer internship had been so successful. And, as detailed in this book's epilogue, I was later pleased to learn how Bob successfully applied his new market segmentation knowledge to the stock market (and how you can, too!).

Chapter 3

Market Research Procedures Class: The "Soup Wars"

A S CLASSES BEGAN, the University of Michigan campus was filled with high hopes for a winning football season. The previous year had failed to produce a Big Ten title, and the pressure was on a new coach to regain the Michigan magic. The first game was with Western Michigan, and expectations were for an easy win. However, Notre Dame was on the horizon, and storm clouds were in sight.

The first Market Research Procedures class session began with the usual formalities. It was good to see Bob in the class along with many students from the Strategic Marketing class. I explained that the pedagogy of the class was to learn by doing. The first several weeks of the class would be an overview of the market research process as explained in my textbook. The course focus was on understanding the process of market research and the methodologies used to identify market facts and information.

The textbook chapters followed the steps of conducting research projects. The beginning chapters dealt with understanding and defining management's need for market information. The bulk of the chapters concerned designing a project and the procedures for analyzing data. The final chapter was on report writing and presentation of findings. Special attention would be given to needs-based market segmentation.

The "doing" part of the class involved a team activity to design and implement a market research project. The textbook was to be used as a reference document to guide students through the steps in the research process. In the past, most projects had involved conducting a survey research project for organizations on and off campus.

THE EVOLUTION OF MARKET SEGMENTATION

Market segmentation has its origin in consumer goods marketing. Firms like Procter & Gamble (P&G) soon recognized that the marketing of one product to the mass market had limitations. By segmenting customers into groups, they found that focusing resources on different groups produced a competitive advantage that increased revenues and lowered costs per sale.

Early segmentation was based on simple demographics such as age, sex, and geographic location. The early success of Ivory Soap's mass-market approach evolved into the development of perfumed soaps targeted to women. Additional market research studies indicated that men preferred a sharp and spicy fragrance. Subsequent studies suggested that the more fundamental difference was not only gender but also basic differences in needs.

P&G's focus on segmenting its markets based on customer needs allowed P&G to quantitatively determine the correlation of need segments with demographic characteristics. If the correlation was high, the demographic characteristic could be used to target the segment with advertising. Consequently, P&G discovered the value of using customer needs as the basis for dividing customers into market segments rather than using demographics.

Business-to-business (B2B) marketers have been much slower in the adoption of needs-based segmentation. Even today, the most common forms of segmentation in B2B marketing are based on simple "firmographics," such as business size, business type, and product usage. Here, the assumption is that large firms like General Motors, General Electric, and Boeing are in the same segment and have similar buying requirements. Failure to recognize that firms differ in the importance placed on delivery times, service support, product specification, and price sensitivity has led to a loss of market share and of competitive advantage for many suppliers.

WHAT ARE BUYER NEEDS?

One perspective is that needs are simply problems buyers have and that they want solved. Buyer needs can be biological, such as need for food, shelter, and sex. They can be social needs, such as having friends and marriage. Needs result from the interaction of people and their environment. Needs are not created by companies. Companies supply the technologies to satisfy needs for a price.

Sony did not create the need for the Walkman; it invented the technology to meet the music needs of customers more conveniently than older music delivery systems. I reminded the class that when buying a drill bit, the buyer does not need a drill bit; he or she needs a hole. Technology could make the drill bit obsolete but not the need for a hole. The Walkman did not create the desire to listen to music. It was a better technology to meet this basic need.

STRATEGIC BENEFITS OF NEEDS-BASED SEGMENTATION

By investing in a needs-based segmentation study, an organization will discover critical information to guide and verify strategic decisions, such as how to truly differentiate its products and services based on important customer needs. The short-run benefits of this investment are realized by focusing marketing, product development, and sales/promotional efforts on high-yield segments. The longer-term benefits build from the construction of a segmentation framework and an organizational culture that can now track changes in the size and dynamics of market structures when necessary.

These benefits allow the organization to quantify market dynamics over time and to plan for changes in product development, manufacturing, and marketing strategy. In addition, the organization can evaluate its competitors' current and potential market strategies. Money spent on needs-based segmentation research is a solid investment in important information that is needed for formulating and maintaining a sustainable competitive advantage.

OVERVIEW OF THE NEEDS-BASED MARKET SEGMENTATION RESEARCH PROCEDURE

Step One: Identify Market Needs

The first step of needs-based market segmentation involves identifying market needs that customers attempt to satisfy when buying goods and services. Market research tools such as focus groups and one-on-one interviews conducted by a professional moderator or interviewer are effective tools for identifying customer needs.

Rarely does a manager or salesperson have the perspective and skills to accomplish this step. Organizations that believe managers inherently know the needs of markets based just on their experience and judgment are making a mistake. Listening to and understanding the needs of your customers require a professional market research approach. It is a rare organization that clearly understands this perspective.

Failure to understand customer needs is the typical cause of losing or not gaining a sustainable competitive advantage. CEOs need to understand that it is the operating manager's responsibility to support market research processes that bring objective and quantitative information regarding customer needs to the organization. Too many managers believe they know what the customer needs based on their personal view of the market. This is reflected in the often-heard comment, "Don't we already know what the customer wants?"

Research suggests that rarely does the manager's perspective match that of the customer. Consumer goods organizations such as P&G have done an excellent job in bringing a proper culture to this issue and are one of the reasons this approach evolved from the consumer goods industry. Following chapters of this book will present examples of "step one" research tools for consumer, service, and business markets. (For further detail about how to conduct this step, please see Appendix B: Class Note—Methodology for Conducting a Needs-Based Segmentation Study.)

Step Two: Segment Customers into Groups

The second step of needs-based market segmentation involves segmenting customers into groups with similar patterns of needs. The critical information from step one is a list of key customer needs identified from the *customer's* perspective, not from management's. It is very important to understand the language of the customer. Rarely is this the language of the organization. Given the list of customer needs, step two involves determining the importance or priority of these needs in the customer's purchase process.

Research suggests there are three generic categories of important needs in consumer, service, and business markets. These three generic groupings are common sense. There is a group of customers whose priority is quality. They are willing to choose goods and services that have superior quality over lower-quality goods or services and to pay a higher price. We call this the "Benefit Segment." A low price is less important to this group and may be a signal to them that the quality of the good or service is low. You can see these customers driving by in their Mercedes-Benz.

The opposite segment is the "Price Segment." These are customers who view lower price as a key trade-off in the purchase process. Walmart and McDonalds clearly are attractive outlets for this price-sensitive group.

The final of the three segments—the middle segment—is the "Benefit/Price Segment." This is a challenging segment since these customers want some degree of quality but at a reasonable price. The critical issue here is to objectively understand the nature of the benefit/price trade-off. Market research procedures such as "preference ranking" and "conjoint measurement" are useful tools to determine the nature of the benefit/price trade-off for all three of the generic groupings. To successfully deliver fact-based information for the organization, these research approaches require professional skills in survey sampling, questionnaire design, and data analysis.

The key deliverable from step two is the presentation of the three generic segments broken out into sub-segments where the market potential or sizes are quantified. This information has critical strategic implications once seen by managers. Following chapters of this book will present the market research methodology used in this step for consumer, service, and business markets.

Step Three: Select Market Target

Once the market structure or "rules or the game" have been quantified, managers can turn to the strategic issues of evaluating and choosing segments to be targeted with products and services. Over time, the monitoring of market needs allows managers to understand the trends in market structure and respond to changing customer needs in order to sustain a competitive advantage.

EXAMPLE OF NEEDS-BASED SEGMENTATION

Figure 3.1 that follows presents the results of a needs-based segmentation study of female investment needs.[1] The study produced three segments:

1. Segment A: Investors who sought investments that outperformed inflation with minimum tax consequences.
2. Segment B: Investors who sought investments that provided capital appreciation with minimal risk.
3. Segment C: Investors who sought investments that produced high levels of current income with minimal risk.

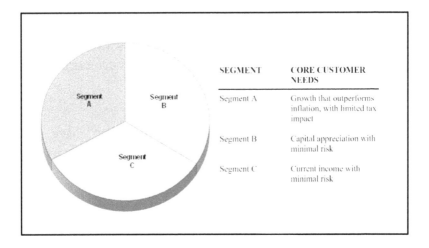

Figure 3.1. Female Investment Market

Given this information, it is not hard to design investment services that best meet the needs of these three segments. However, how can we identify which females are in which segment?

The next step in the segmentation process is to determine which identifying characteristics differentiate one segment of customers from another based on demographic, economic, lifestyle, and behavioral characteristics. Table 3.1 that follows presents the results of this analysis. Based on this information, marketing programs can be targeted to each of these market segments.

Segment Profile	Career Woman	Single Parent	Mature Woman
Segment Needs	Growth that out-performs inflation, with limited tax consequences	Capital appreciation with minimal risk	Current income with minimal risk
Demographics			
• Age	35-55	35-55	55-75
• Income > $50,000	86%	3%	63%
• Working	100%	43%	17%
• Professional	83%	9%	13%
• Married	56%	13%	35%
• Youngest Child <15	24%	83%	5%
• College Educated	78%	23%	17%
Lifestyle			
• Investment Attitude	Confident	Concerned	Conservative
• Interests	Sports/Reading	Family	Leisure
• Entertainment	Concerts	Movies	Television
• Key Value	Individualistic	Cooperative	Traditional
Use Behaviors			
• Experience	Some/Extensive	None/Limited	Moderate
• Risk Preference	Moderate/High	Low	Moderate
• Net Worth	Growing	Fixed	Fixed

Table 3.1. Customer Characteristics of the Female Investor Market Segment

EVALUATING THE COST OF RESEARCH

A considerable level of professional effort and resources is required to implement a meaningful segmentation study. Organizations that have not used market research often react to the absolute cost of the study with concern. A typical reaction is, "Can't we do this cheaper?" Like all business decisions, the cost of the research should be evaluated from a cost–benefit perspective.

Consider the following example:

- Cost of segmentation study: $100,000
- Market size under study: 10,000,000 units/year
- Sales price: $20/unit
- Variable cost: $15/unit

- First year breakeven: $100,000/\$5 = 20,000$ units
- Breakeven (B/E) share of market (SOM): .002%

The issue for management is whether the information from the segmentation study provides enough strategic leverage to increase market share by .002%. If not, the money should not be spent on the research study. Note that if the research cost is doubled to $200,000, the market share breakeven increases to only .004%. $200,000 can buy a very respectable needs-based research study.

However, there is still another perspective on this issue. The previous example assumes that the strategic leverage gained from the study ends in one year. If this is not the case, the B/E SOM in year two is .001% for the $100,000 cost. Viewed from this financial perspective, researchers have encountered managers who ask if they are spending enough to ensure they have the greatest strategy leverage from the study. Consequently, the cost of research is rarely a barrier to conducting a needs-based segmentation study once the financial leverage is understood.

At this point, the central learning lesson for the class was that strategic leverage is discovered by defining markets from the perspective of "needs-based market segmentation"—a technique developed by leading packaged-goods firms and later applied to business and service markets. While this approach has been used by several leading businesses over the last few years, many businesses are not aware of the strategic advantage that fact-based needs segmentation can bring to their businesses.

STUDENT MARKET RESEARCH PROJECT

A major part of the students' grade for the Market Research Procedures course would involve a team research project. Teams of four or five were to be formed. Each was responsible for designing a research project and completing it during the semester. A written report and presentation to the class were required. Team formations were to be reported at the next class.

Bob and three other students formed a team. They scheduled a team meeting in a conference room to discuss potential projects. Each person suggested project ideas, but the one presented by Ashley Stone seemed the best. Her summer internship had involved an interesting competitive challenge for Campbell Soup, and her project related to that experience.

The group scheduled a second meeting where Ashley could present more details of the project. Her summer position had been a job in the test kitchens of Campbell. The test kitchens formulated new products and conducted taste tests to evaluate consumer acceptance. Ashley was assigned to the project team coordinating product testing with the marketing group in charge of the ready-to-serve soup line. She was immediately involved in conducting taste tests for Campbell's line of thicker ready-to-serve soups. The line was called "Chunky."

The Chunky line of soups controlled 61% of the market. Its leading competitor was Progresso, with 24% of the market. The Progresso brand was owned by the Pillsbury Company of Minneapolis, Minnesota. Pillsbury had recently announced it was taking the offensive with a comparative advertising campaign that attacked Campbell's older condensed soup line. Progresso sold only ready-to-serve soup, which competed directly with Campbell's Chunky line of ready-to-serve soups. Progresso's strategy was to switch adults from Campbell's condensed line of soups to Progresso's thicker soups by focusing on the adult market's "preference" for thicker soups.

In a TV spot being aired by Progresso, a woman walks into a kitchen where a young man is eating a bowl of Chicken & Stars, with a red and white can with the word "Condensed" written in Campbell's signature script displayed prominently beside the bowl. "Hey there, big brother, what are you eating? You know, Chicken & Stars used to be my favorite. Then I learned to ride a two-wheeler. Come on; you're an adult now. There's a better-tasting soup."

The taste preference resonates even more strongly in Progresso's print ads. The ads show a bowl of Campbell's condensed chicken noodle soup, identified by name, next to a bowl of Progresso's white chicken noodle soup (as shown in Figure 3.2 that follows). Because Progresso only makes ready-to-serve soups, the Campbell comparison isn't exactly apples to apples. Within the industry, Progresso is considered to compete mainly with Campbell's ready-to-serve Chunky soup.

Figure 3.2. Progresso Comparative Print Advertisement

The previous ten years had been a period of level and then declining sales for Campbell's condensed clam chowder soup. Campbell attributed this decline in sales to the success of Campbell's Chunky ready-to-serve (RTS) clam chowder and the competitive battle with Progresso's RTS clam chowder. In addition, private-label condensed soups like Fisherman's Delight clam chowder had impacted Campbell's condensed soup franchise. Fisherman's Delight was a privately-branded condensed soup distributed by a leading national supermarket chain. It was positioned as a price competitor to Campbell's condensed soup line. Progresso's positioning was quite different. Its strategy was to differentiate Progresso from Campbell's traditional condensed soup line by offering the customers a thicker RTS soup. This strategy built on the growing market for RTS soups.

The Campbell marketing group recognized that Campbell's RTS soups faced a serious competitive threat from the private labels of national supermarket chains and the direct competition from Progresso. While these competitive threats were pervasive to the complete Campbell line of condensed and RTS soups, the group decided to focus attention on Campbell's clam chowder as a pilot test to better understand the competitive positioning of condensed and RTS soups in the adult marketplace. Clam chowder was selected since children are not users of the condensed version of Campbell's clam chowder.

The brand manager for Campbell's Chunky soup line was assigned to be the research project leader. A New York City research firm was contacted regarding a consumer test of the adult soup market in Boston. After several meetings, the research firm recommended that a series of focus group interviews be conducted with current users of the three chowder brands (Campbell, Progresso, and Fisherman's Delight) in order to explore reasons for product usage, reactions to the brands, and perceived product differences. Through focus group sessions of this nature, the research firm believed that the cause of declining sales of Campbell's chowder franchise could be explored and potential solutions identified.

The results of the focus group sessions suggested that the thickness of clam chowder was an important attribute in brand selection. Of the former Campbell's chowder users, the desire for a thicker formulation was the predominant reason for switching.

Many of these chowder users had switched to either Campbell's Chunky chowder or Progresso's chowder. Several users indicated the lower price of Fisherman's Delight chowder influenced their switching, in addition to the thickness.

Based on these findings, the research firm recommended that a taste test be conducted to determine the actual preference levels for Campbell's two clam chowders (condensed and Chunky RTS) and for the soups of the two competitors, Progresso and Fisherman's Delight. It was suggested that a new clam chowder RTS formulation be developed for the taste test, which was somewhat less thick than Campbell's and Progresso's RTS formulations. Comments by several focus group participants indicated that the thickness of Campbell's and Progresso's RTS formulations should be somewhat less thick. None of the comments indicated that the formulations should be thicker. This new formulation would be evaluated in a taste test along with Campbell's current chowders plus the two competitive brands.

After several meetings on specific aspects of the proposed research design, the product manager decided to approve the project. Ashley worked with the research lab to develop a "less thick" formulation of Chunky clam chowder.

Campbell's Research Study

Ashley explained that she was not directly involved in the Campbell research study design or data analysis but would do her best to recall what she could. She believed the design involved about two hundred respondents. The sample was split, with half male and half female canned chowder users. The subjects were selected using a probability sampling procedure involving a telephone-administered qualifying questionnaire.

Since Ashley was directly involved in administering the taste test part of the study, she explained the process in detail. The subjects came to one of four test locations (local churches). They tested individually in thirty-minute sessions. Subjects were brought into the testing room and seated at stalls. An instruction sheet explained that the subject was to evaluate several samples of chowder, that the test would consist of three parts, and that they would be required to taste a total of fifteen cups of chowder. Normal taste-testing procedures were followed.

The first part of the test involved a subject tasting five samples of chowder and ranking them from "most preferred" to "least preferred." The five chowders were Campbell condensed chowder (Thin), Fisherman's Delight condensed chowder (Thin), Campbell's new RTS formulation (Thick), Progresso's RTS chowder (Extra Thick), and Campbell RTS chowder (Extra Thick).

The second and third parts of the test involved tasting five samples again. The samples had different code letters, and the subjects were not told the samples were *identical* to the previous five. After tasting the five samples, the subjects were again asked to rank-order the five samples.

For each subject, the test procedure resulted in three preference orderings of the five chowder samples. The preference orderings were combined to form a composite ordering for each subject—a procedure that resulted in a more reliable measure of each subject's true preference ordering.

The findings of the research study were presented at a meeting of the Campbell's project team. Ashley had never received a copy of the report, so she did her best to recall the main findings of the presentation. The data set was analyzed by calculating the average rank order of each chowder formulation and scaling the chowders on a five-point scale ranging from most preferred to least preferred. Ashley remembered the results being as follow, in Table 3.2.

Most Preferred:	Campbell's New RTS Formulation (Thick)
	Fisherman's Delight Condensed (Thin)
	Progresso's RTS (Extra Thick)
	Campbell's Condensed (Thin)
Least Preferred:	Campbell's RTS (Extra Thick)

Table 3.2. Most Preferred to Least Preferred Chowders
(Ashley's Recollection)

The research objectives for the taste test were to develop a competitive strategy to counter the sales decline of the Campbell clam chowder franchise. Specifically, to explore product line strategies that would defend and grow the franchise. Study recommendations were as follow:

1. Drop Campbell's condensed clam chowder, which is clearly not preferred by adult clam chowder users and is inconsistent with the trend toward convenient, RTS soups.
2. Change the formulation of the current Campbell's Chunky RTS soup to the new formulation (which is less thick than Progresso RTS). Communicate this formulation change to adult chowder users with a new label, which makes this change conspicuous at point of purchase. In addition, aggressively attack Progresso with a comparative taste test campaign demonstrating the superior taste preference for the new formulation over Progresso RTS clam chowder.

The research indicated that the current formulations of Campbell's Chunky RTS clam chowder and Campbell's condensed clam chowder ranked significantly below the two competitors' brands. This preference disadvantage was a key driver in the decline in Campbell's share of market in the clam chowder space. However, Campbell's new RTS clam chowder formulation was preferred over Progresso's current RTS clam chowder. The difference in rating was statistically significant at the .05 level. The new formulation offered Campbell a competitive differential advantage over Progresso on a key dimension of choice in the purchase of clam chowder soup.

Ashley recalled the heated discussion at Campbell that followed the presentation of the findings. There was a group in the marketing department that clearly opposed the recommendations. The research firm was aggressively grilled as to the validity of the results. At this point, Ashley said she had to leave the meeting for another scheduled meeting.

Ashley later learned that Campbell's VP of Marketing had reviewed the research results and recommendations. It was reported that a Wharton Business School professor who specialized in quantitative marketing research would be consulted. Ashley learned that the professor believed the data analysis was incorrect, and his consulting firm would reanalyze the data. With her summer internship coming to an end, Ashley was not privy to the new recommendations.

Student Team's Taste Test

Ashley's idea for her team's Market Research Procedures class research project was to replicate the Campbell research study on a small scale and explore alternative ways to analyze the data. She would try to contact friends at Campbell who might have some information on how the Wharton professor reanalyzed the data. Otherwise, they would use the various approaches presented in the class's market research textbook. I approved the group's research study, and they started to work on the project.

The team divided up responsibilities for the research project. Ashley was the project manager and would design the taste testing procedures. Bob would make arrangements for a room in which to conduct the testing and would acquire the materials and chowder products. Other team members would find and screen students and others who would be used for the testing. All of the team members would be involved in tabulating the data and exploring alternative methods for its analysis.

The data collection was completed by the end of October. Fifty-two students and business school employees had participated in the taste test. Approximately half were male and half female, like the Campbell study. The same chowder products were tested, and Ashley was able to formulate a "less thick" Chunky product, like that used in the Campbell study. Figure 3.3 that follows shows the three national brands used in the taste test.

Figure 3.3. National Brands Tested

The team's initial data analysis followed that used in the Campbell study, averaging the rank orders. Table 3.3 that follows presents the results. The results appeared to be like those reported by Ashley from her recollection of the Campbell study.

Customers	Campbell's Condensed	Fisherman's Delight	Campbell's New	Progresso	Campbell's Chunky
	Thin	Somewhat Thin	Moderate Thickness	Thick	Very Thick
1	1	2	3	4	5
2	2	1	3	4	5
3	1	2	3	4	5
4	5	4	3	2	1
5	5	4	3	2	1
6	5	4	1	2	3
7	1	2	3	4	5
8	5	4	3	2	1
9	1	2	3	4	5
10	5	4	3	2	1
11	3	1	2	4	5
12	5	2	1	3	4
13	5	4	3	1	2
14	5	3	1	2	4
15	1	2	3	4	5
16	1	2	3	4	5
17	5	4	2	1	3
18	3	2	1	4	5
19	5	4	3	2	1
20	4	2	1	3	5
N	20	20	20	20	20
Mean	3.4	2.8	2.4	2.9	3.6
Std. Dev.	1.8	1.1	.9	1.1	1.7

Table 3.3. Preference Orderings of Five Clam Chowders (Need Priority)

Reviewing Table 3.3, Campbell's RTS Chunky and Condensed soups had the lowest ratings among those tested. The difference between the two Campbell soups and the competitors Progressive RTS and Fisherman's Condensed was large. This clearly supported the conclusion to drop Campbell's condensed product and reformulate Chunky with the new formulation. The promotional budget for the dropped condensed brand could be used to aggressively introduce the new formulation of Chunky. The recommendation of the Campbell's research study seemed to be on solid ground.

At this point, the team decided to take a closer look at the individual preference data. Table 3.3 presented the random selection of twenty students' preference orderings. It was disturbing to look at the variation in the preference orderings. For example, if Campbell's condensed were dropped, five students with a first-order preference would not be happy. On the other hand, nine students clearly didn't prefer the condensed formulation. It seems like there is a love–hate situation in the market.

Further inspection of Table 3.3 revealed that the six testers who preferred Campbell's condensed brand all disliked Campbell's RTS Chunky brand. And the nine testers who disliked Campbell's condensed brand had very high preferences for Campbell's RTS Chunky and Progresso's RTS formulations. The data clearly supports the observation in Campbell's focus groups that customers' preferences were related to the thickness of the soup formation. Some customers like thin soups (condensed), and other customers prefer thicker formulations like Campbell's RTS Chunky and Progresso's RTS. What does this say regarding the recommendation to drop Campbell's condensed brand and RTS Chunky?

Table 3.3 suggests that dropping Campbell's condensed would result in current Campbell customers switching to Fisherman's Delight over time since Fisherman's Delight is customers' second preference after Campbell's condensed. The same is true for Campbell's RTS Chunky formulation. Progresso's RTS formulation is the second preference of customers who had a first preference for the Campbell's chunky formulation. Dropping Campbell's Chunky product would result in current Campbell customers switching to Progresso's RTS product over time.

Consequently, this line of reasoning suggests that the best way to defend against Progresso's competitive advances is to keep both Campbell's condensed and Chunky RTS products and introduce Campbell's new RTS formulation, which has a clear preference advantage over the Progresso formulation. Only two customers preferred Progresso over Campbell's new formulation. This product line strategy would stabilize Campbell's current market position and grow its share over time with an innovative marketing program to attack Progresso's market share.

How could the conclusions of the market research report be so different than the reanalysis just completed? The answer appears to be that there are segments in the soup market that prefer different benefits in the soups. Clearly, customer needs differ in the soup market, just as they did in the chemical toilet market we looked at in Chapter 2. The appropriate approach for the market research study would have been to use a needs-based segmentation approach in analyzing customers' preferences.

The class team contacted Rajah, my Ph.D. student, for help in using the cluster analysis program (discussed in Chapter 2) to reanalyze the data. The reanalysis of the data using the needs-based segmentation approach is presented in Figure 3.4 that follows.

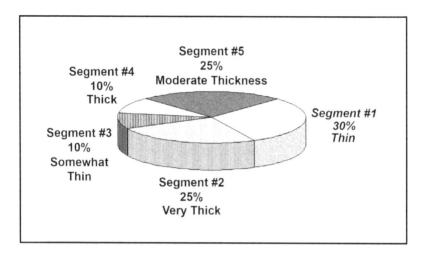

Figure 3.4. Chowder Market Segments (First Choice)

The result of the cluster analysis indicates that the adult soup market is composed of five segments. Among those segments, a large group of 30% prefers "thin" soup, another large group of 25% prefers "very thick" soup, and another large group of 25% prefers "moderate thickness." Campbell's condensed clam chowder is positioned in the large "thin" soup segment and has historically had a dominant share of market in this segment.

The recommendation to drop the condensed product was clearly misguided, given the reanalysis of the data. The entry of Campbell's Chunky chowder soup and Progresso's soup into the "very thick" and "moderate thickness" segments was a successful positioning strategy by both companies and resulted in the erosion of market share away from Campbell's condensed product. The strategic insight from the reanalyzed data is the strong positioning of Campbell's new formulation into the large "moderate thickness" segment. This positioning would capture customers who had purchased Campbell's chunky and Progresso's thicker soups. However, the research indicates that Progresso would be the big loser in this share loss.

The student team completed the research report in early December and made its presentation to the class. The class projects were graded by members of the class in a secret ballot. The team was delighted to get the highest grade and took Ashley out to dinner for her great project idea and her effort in making the project a winner.

The class came away from the project with new insights on market research studies, including two main insights. First, it is easy to be strategically misled by such studies if an improper data analysis is used. Markets are composed of customer segments and averaging across segments can be very deceptive. There is an old story about a cowboy approaching a river. He asks an Indian how deep the river is. The Indian, with a smile, says, "one inch on average." The cowboy drowns in an eight-foot hole. Second, needs-based segmentation is a way to look strategically forward in a business rather than backward (backward being the case with financial data). Future opportunities and problems can be identified with fact-based segmentation data. It is a valuable forecasting tool.

The Actual Results of Campbell's Research Study

Basically, Campbell's new formulation, named Campbell's Select (shown in Figure 3.5 that follows), was positioned on the less thick side of Progresso while Campbell's Chunky was positioned on the thicker side of Progresso. The result was a slowing of Progresso's market share gain.

Figure 3.5. Campbell's New Formulation: "Campbell's Select"

The Campbell research study, like our student project, discovered important information regarding the background characteristics of customer segments. Females typically prefer thinner soups, while males prefer thicker soups. This information was central to understanding the target market and designing the value proposition for promotional programs. Campbell implemented an advertising campaign targeting Chunky RTS soups to men, using sports stars who profess to eat only thick soups. Monday Night Football often featured famous football stars eating Campbell's Chunky soup served up by their mothers.

The new formulation Campbell's Select (a moderately thick formulation) was targeted to men *and* women. Here, the advertising shows a housewife eating her favorite soup, Campbell's Select, and having her husband try a taste. Of course, he loves it.

The "thin" soup segment retained a focus on women eating their favorite soup, Campbell Condensed. Children were frequently featured eating their favorite, Chicken Noodle, with Mom. Dad is never to be seen in these advertisements.

Later, Campbell strengthened its market lead in the $3.9 billion US soup market with a 59% share of the US ready-to-serve market. Progresso has made impressive gains but remains a distant Number 2 to Campbell in the ready-to-serve market, with a 24% share of the market. Other brands in the category were hit hard by the aggressive marketing effort of Campbell and Progresso, losing share down to 17%. The competitive attack of Progresso was successfully challenged, and Campbell's differential advantage defended. However, Progresso established itself as a strong competitor to Campbell, and both competitors focused on innovative target market strategies in the years ahead.

Chapter 4

MBA Field Project: Mobil Oil

IN THIS CHAPTER, we will again see the value of the needs-based segmentation process, this time in the unexpected context of a market generally considered to be commoditized—that is, driven primarily by price. The final year of the University of Michigan's MBA program requires teams of students to apply what they have learned to a real business problem. Firms were contacted and screened by Michigan's Ross School of Business for projects in marketing, finance, human resources, and operations management.

The projects required the students to be at the organizations' facilities for the duration of the project. Many projects were worldwide and offered students practical consulting experience as well as foreign travel. Faculty advisors were assigned to the teams, and I felt fortunate to be involved with the Mobil Oil project, which only required travel to Chicago.

The team assigned to the Mobil project included students who had taken the Marketing Strategy and Market Research Procedures course. The Mobil project required the students to develop a written strategic marketing plan and to participate in its implementation. (For a definition of "Strategic Marketing Planning," see Appendix C: Terminology Used in This Book.) The plan was to be fact-based, using the information supplied from a consulting project recently conducted by Mobil as well as from focus group interviews Mobil conducted with consumers of gasoline and related products. The consulting project included an extensive needs-based segmentation study. The following is an overview of the students' final report.

STUDENTS' MOBIL OIL REPORT

The student team's first task was to review the consulting report. The report began by stating that Mobil was confronted by a classic issue that most organizations are confronted with: the commoditization of their market, where price is the main criterion in the purchase process. According to conventional wisdom, all markets follow a cycle of growth and maturity, then commoditization and decline. In a true commodity market, price is the only differentiator. Such might seem to be the case in the automotive gasoline market. Gasoline is gasoline, so why not buy from the station that has the lowest price? This commodity perspective can easily be the mindset of the seller when the focus is on the similarity of the products being sold.

The consulting report argued that Mobil Oil Company was confronted with this commoditization perspective and needed to change its organizational culture from a product orientation to a customer-driven orientation. Key to this change was developing a formal strategic marketing plan and implementing a needs-based market segmentation study of the automotive gasoline market.

Mobil's corporate objective should be to significantly increase operating cash flow and become the industry's profit leader. In the past, poor financial performance had resulted in weak stock prices and growing shareholder dissatisfaction with the company's management. The consulting report indicated there were two basic levers to accomplish Mobil's objective: revenue growth and productivity improvement.

The revenue growth lever had two components: (1) build the business franchise with revenue from new markets, new products, and new customers; and (2) increase the value to existing customers by deepening relationships with them through expanded sales—for example, cross-selling products or offering bundled products instead of single products. The productivity lever also had two parts: (1) improve the company's cost structure by reducing direct and indirect expenses, and (2) use assets more efficiently by reducing the working and fixed capital needed to support a given business level.[1]

The consultant's recommendation for a strategic vision statement for Mobil was "to be the best integrated refiner-marketer in the United States by efficiently delivering unprecedented value to customers." (For a definition and examples of "Vision Statement," see Appendix C: Terminology Used in This Book.) Also, the mission statement was "to increase [Mobil's] return on capital employed by more than six percentage points within three years." (For a definition and examples of "Mission Statement," see Appendix C: Terminology Used in This Book.) To achieve this level of performance, major organizational changes would be required. It is no small matter to achieve revenue growth and to drive performance through productivity improvement at the same time.

A key strategic point in the consulting report emphasized that Mobil did not sell directly to final consumers. The company's immediate customer was the independent owner of gasoline stations. These franchised retailers purchased gasoline and other products from Mobil and sold them to consumers in Mobil-branded stations. Mobil's management must, the report pointed out, recognize that competitive differentiation occurs at the dealer location, not at Mobil's own manufacturing and distribution facilities. Consequently, effective relationships with Mobil's franchised retailers became central to successful strategy changes in the future.

The report advised Mobil that an investment in efforts to improve productivity usually yields profit results sooner than an investment in efforts to grow revenue. Financial benefits from improved business processes typically reveal themselves in stages. Firstly, cost savings from increased operational efficiencies and process improvements create near-term benefits. Secondly, revenue growth from enhanced customer relationships accrues in the intermediate term, and thirdly, increased innovation can also produce long-term revenue and margin improvements.

Mobil's previous strategic approach to the market was very similar to that of its major competitors. In the past, Mobil had attempted to sell a full range of gasoline products and services to all consumers while still matching the low prices of nearby discount stations. Maintaining volume in the face of severe price competition was a central concern of Mobil executives. Gasoline was viewed as a commodity product by management, and customers were perceived as basically all alike. The industry had evolved into a competitive environment based on price competition. Competitive margins had declined over the years, and the "gasoline business" was considered to be a mature commodity nightmare by most managers.

MARKET RESEARCH PROJECT

The research consultants advised Mobil that their perception of customers should be evaluated through a program of marketing research studies. The first phase of this research program involved a series of focus groups with consumers of gasoline and related products, conducted across the United States. It was recommended that ten focus groups, composed of nine to twelve consumers, be conducted across the United States. This included consumers who purchased from Mobil stations as well as from competitors.

The focus group research phase took a month to complete. The results convinced management that their view of the consumers as being "all alike" was not based in reality. Consumers expressed great diversity regarding the importance of price, quality of products and services, issues of convenience regarding pumping gas, desire for related products such as soft drinks and snacks, and methods of payment. In addition, consumers exhibited differences in needs based on gender, employment status, age, income, driving habits, and geographic location.

In reviewing the results, the student team referenced their classroom discussion (as presented in Chapter 3 of this book) that all markets are composed of three generic segments. There is one group of customers who place high importance on the quality of products and services, including on brand image and the prestige of ownership. This group is called the "Benefit Segment." This group may even use higher price as a cue that the products/services are superior.

The second group of customers is price shoppers, who place high importance on low prices. This group is called the "Price Segment." They are looking for products/services that are on sale. "Black Friday" is a special day for them.

The third group of customers makes trade-offs between lower price and the quality of products/services. This group is called the "Benefit/Price Segment." They go through a juggling process of trading off product features against the added price of the product.

The focus group results suggested that all three generic segments were operating in the consumer gasoline market. The results of the ten focus groups identified the following five summary categories of customer gasoline purchase needs:

- High quality/branded products and services
- Fast and convenient service and quality products
- Convenient location of the station
- Low price of gasoline
- Availability of a convenience store

The next phase of the consumer research program involved a survey research project designed to quantitatively measure the importance of these potential need categories using formal market research procedures. This phase took over three months to complete. Over 2,000 telephone interviews were conducted with consumers of gasoline across the United States. The central issue was the preference ranking of these five primary needs categories.

Table 4.1 that follows presents the results of this research. The five needs categories had clear differences in their importance. The five groups were given the names of True Blues, Road Warriors, Generation F3, Home Bodies, and Price Shoppers.[2]

(1 — Most Important, 5 — Least Important)

Core Customer Needs	True Blues	Road Warriors	Generation F3	Home Bodies	Price Shoppers
Quality Product/ Service	1	2	5	2	4
Fast Service/ Quality Products	2	1	4	3	5
Convenience of Location	4	4	2	1	3
Low Price	5	5	3	4	1
Convenience store	3	3	1	5	2

Table 4.1. Importance Ordering of Core Customer Needs

In reviewing the results, the student team first compared the similarity of the rank orders of the five market segments. Note that True Blues and Road Warriors have very similar preference orderings. The only difference is the reversal of the first and second preference ordering. Both segments see price as not important. Clearly, these two segments could be combined to form the generic "Benefit Segment." Of the remaining three segments, the Price Shoppers segment is distinctive in that low price is most important in their purchase decision process. This customer group is the generic "Price Segment." The remaining two groups, Generation F3 and Home Bodies, have somewhat similar preference orderings, and we would place them in the third generic trade-off segment, called the "Benefit/Price Segment." Price is third and fourth in importance to them.

Table 4.2 that follows presents the five market segments and their most important needs (as reported in Table 4.1).

SEGMENT	CORE CUSTOMER NEEDS
Road Warriors	Fast service and quality products
Generation F3	Fuel, fast food
True Blues	Quality products and service
Home Bodies	Convenient location, trustworthy
Price Shoppers	Low price

Table 4.2. Top Core Customer Needs by Segment

Table 4.3 that follows presents the five segments and their market size. Market size was the proportion of customers in each segment. Note that this is not the same as dollar market potential since some customer segments could use more gas per person than other segments. Table 4.3 also completes the segmentation process by determining the association of demographic, behavioral, and attitude characteristics to the five segments.

Segment	Size	Core Customer Needs	Use Behavior and Attitudes	Key Demographics
Road Warriors	16%	Quality Products and Quality Service	Drives 25,000 to 50,000 miles a year; buys premium gas, drinks, and sandwiches; drives late model expensive car; likes technology; pays at the pump with credit card; brand and sometimes station loyal.	Higher income; mainly middle-aged businessmen; college educated
Generation F3	27%	Fast Fuel and Food	Drives 15,000 to 20,000 miles; constantly on the go; frequent driver; heavy user of snack food and drinks; many smoke; older cars and trucks.	Upwardly mobile men and women; half under 25; many single; middle income; high school/college education
True Blues	16%	Fast Service and Quality Products	Drives 15,000 to 35,000 miles a year; brand and sometimes station loyal; buys premium gas; pays cash and uses credit card	Men and women with moderate to high income; middle-aged and older; college educated.
Home Bodies	21%	Convenient Station Location and Trustworthy	Drives 7,000 to 12,000 miles a year; uses whatever gasoline is conveniently located when tank is low; likes trusting safe location.	Usually housewives who shuttle children around during day in a van/SUV; middle and high income.
Price Shoppers	20%	Low Price	Drives 10,000 to 30,000 miles a year; thinks he/she is a smart shopper; neither brand nor station loyal and rarely buy premium gas; older cars and trucks.	Male and female; usually on tight budgets; high school educated

Table 4.3. Mobil Corporation Segmentation Scheme and Segment Profiles

The primary insight provided by the segmentation study was that only 20% of customers who purchase gasoline were price-sensitive (spent $700/yr.) and 80% considered other things to be of more importance than price (spent $1,200/yr.). This suggests that the price-sensitive segment is smaller than the 20% reported in Table 4.3. Clearly, Mobil's previous perception that the market for consumer gasoline was a commodity business where price dominated the consumer's purchase decision was false.

Mobil executives recognized that the opportunity to differentiate the company from the competition occurs at the dealer locations, not at its manufacturing facilities, which basically produce commodity products (gasoline, heating oil, and jet fuel). Consequently, management's focus turned to understanding the non-price attributes important to customers in purchasing gasoline and to understanding the differences in the use behavior and demographics of the price and non-price segments of the gasoline marketplace.

DEVELOPING A MARKETING STRATEGY

For the first time, Mobil had fact-based market information regarding the "rules of the game" in the retail gasoline market. The voice of the customer was clearly at the forefront of the strategic thinking in Mobil's top management. Management no longer had to use their personal perceptions of the market as the basis for formulating a marketing strategy.

The students stated that marketing strategy is composed of four interdependent decisions. They are: (1) target market selection, (2) target competitor selection, (3) determining the value proposition, and (4) determining the aggressiveness of the marketing program. The students' strategic market plan covered these four areas.

1. Target Market Selection

Table 4.3 presented the profiles of the five market segments. Which market segments should be the focus of Mobil's marketing strategy? What emphasis should be placed on the segments? It was clear that the market attractiveness of the five segments differed in strategic importance.

The "Benefit Segments" of Road Warriors and True Blues represented 32% of the customer base but significantly more in terms of market potential. These two segments drive more miles per year and used premium gas to a higher degree than the other segments. These two segments spent as much as $1,200 annually on gasoline compared to the Price Segment, which spent $700 annually. This difference in usage raised the dollar market potential of the benefit segments to nearly 43%. Clearly, these two segments represent a significant market opportunity and became a primary target for Mobil's marketing efforts.

The "Benefit/Price Segments" of Generation F3 and Home Bodies represented a somewhat less attractive market. However, Generation F3 was the more attractive of the two. It was the largest of the segments in customer size. A convenience store was more important to this group, which represented an opportunity to expand Mobil's product line to include new profit centers. This segment was more price-sensitive than the "Benefit Segment" and desired mid-grade (special) or regular gasoline. However, Generation F3 drove as many miles as the True Blue segment, which represented significant revenue volume. The market potential of this segment was estimated to be 30%.

The "Price Segment" was considered least attractive, given the customers' preference for low margin price gasoline (regular) even though they drove a significant number of miles per year. The market potential was estimated to be less than 20%.

Given this analysis of the segment dollar market potential, Mobil selected the True Blue and Road Warrior segments as the primary target and Generation F3 as the secondary target. These top three segments became the focus of a new Mobil marketing strategy. Greater financial performance could be expected since these segments produce higher revenue per customer because they buy more gas, premium products, and food products. In addition, the average margin per customer in each of these segments is also higher because the products they buy often have higher margins. By focusing on these three segments, the company implemented a series of marketing strategies to better serve their needs. If successful, Mobil could expect to grow its revenue and profits.

2. Target Competitor Selection

Mobil recognized that the target competitors would remain the other premium brands, such as Exxon, Shell, and Chevron. However, the change in marketing strategy would not consider discount stations as competitors. This would mean the participation in price wars would be deemphasized.

3. Value Proposition Development

The student report emphasized that the core of any marketing strategy is the value proposition. This refers to the positioning of the marketing program in the target consumer's mind, relative to competitive products. The value proposition identifies the key reason(s) that will motivate customers to purchase from your organization rather than from competitors. It defines how the organization will differentiate itself to attract, retain, and deepen relationships with targeted customers.

This statement of how the organization proposes to deliver superior value to customers should be the firm's single most important organizing principle. It must be based on organizational skills and resources that deliver value as perceived by the customer. The value proposition is crucial because it helps an organization connect its internal processes to improved outcomes for its customers.

Mobil developed a value proposition targeting the needs of both the Benefit Segments (Road Warriors and True Blues) and the needs of the Benefit/Price Segment (Generation F3). Table 4.2

made it clear that Mobil must develop marketing programs that satisfy the important needs of quality products/services delivered fast (Benefit Segment) and provide the products and services of a convenience store at easy access locations (Benefit/Price Segment).

4. Aggressive Organizational Changes

Mobil had previously approved aggressive organizational changes to its marketing department. New positions were to be added as part of the move to a more customer-oriented culture. Positions such as Manager of Marketing Development, Manager of Training and Sales Force Development, Manager of Consumer Research, and Manager of Franchise Development expanded the capabilities of the Marketing Department to formulate and implement the new marketing strategy.

Central to the changes was the development of new positions based on Mobil's new value proposition. Four managers were charged with developing and implementing programs and processes focused on the customer needs of friendly service ("smiles"), recognition/loyalty ("strokes"), fast-in-and-out ("speed"), and convenience stores.

Smile Team Leader: The mission of this job was to create a station environment where self-service is delivered with a smile. This involved greeting people and helping them out and showing customers that Mobil appreciates their business and wants them to come back.

Strokes Team Leader: The mission of this job was to reward Mobil's best customers. The best way to recognize the best customers is not necessarily at the station but rather through direct mail. The goal was to get these customers into Mobil's database, monitor their behavior, and communicate with them through direct mail efforts for upgrades to higher-quality products, special privileges, and special thank you communications.

Speed Team Leader: The focus of this job was to look at every detailed step in the buying process, from the time a customer comes on to the lot until they leave. It required breaking down each step in the process and looking to see how Mobil could make it easier for the customer. This involved looking at the credit card process and how to make it easier at the pump. It also involved looking at vehicle identification technology and distributing toll tags for vehicles. Putting people out on the island to accept cash would be evaluated, as would the possibility of having a touch screen at the pump to automate service and make it simple and fast.

Manager Franchise Development: The market research study found that 90% of Mobil customers shop at convenience stores, but only 10% shop at Mobil station convenience stores. The obvious conclusion for Mobil was that something was wrong with its stores. To study this problem, Mobil built models of various convenience store designs, to study what customers wanted when shopping in a real store environment. Its goal was to become the alternative to the express checkout line at a supermarket.

DEVELOPING TACTICAL MARKETING PROGRAMS

Mobil again turned to consumer research as a tool to provide management with input and feedback on tactical ideas and programs designed to meet target segment needs. The needs-based segmentation study (Table 4.3) provided researchers with the "Use Behavior" and "Key Demographics" of the Road Warriors,

True Blues, and Generation F3 target segments. Several focus groups sessions were held with each of the three target segments.

The objective of the focus group sessions was to gain a deeper understanding of the needs of each segment and to explore ideas on how Mobil could best meet their needs. The sessions were seen as a creative tool to explore innovative concepts and gain a customer perspective on such ideas. Each of the four managers previously discussed was responsible for the focus groups and for developing proposals to deliver and execute tactical programs better than their competition.

The strategy development team recognized that the key to executing its strategy was to have employees clearly understand it. Unfortunately, many employees failed to appreciate the importance of a clear and complete understanding of the strategy. When the strategy development team attempted to implement the strategy, it gave only limited descriptions of what employees should do and why those tasks are important. Without clear and more detailed information, such as that provided in a needs-based segmentation study, it's no wonder that many companies have failed in executing their strategies. After all, how can employees carry out a plan they don't fully understand?

Mobil recognized this issue and developed special seminars to educate employees on the change in strategy, using a video that explained the needs-based segmentation study. The text that follows is a transcript of the customer-need comments by market segment. The video was a powerful tool in communicating the voice of the customer to employees and to the distribution channel of gas stations.

Mobil Oil Video Transcript (Selected Comments)

ROAD WARRIORS: Primary Need Is Quality Gas Products/ Services

Female: "The brand of gas is important to me. If it is a major brand, I will stop for gas."

Male: "I buy premium gas for my BMW, wouldn't take a chance on a cut-rate station."

Male: "I travel to work and stop at the same station. It is a hassle to deal with different pumps."

Female: "I pay with cash at our local station. The person at the cash register is very nice."

Male: "I only stop at a _____ station. I like their gas."

Female: "The major stations have quality gas. I don't want to have engine problems."

Male: "I have been with _____ for many years, and I am not about to make any changes."

Male: "You can go down the road and all of these new little places have opened up. Bob's Service Station and Small Appliance Repair has a cheaper rate on gasoline, and I am not going to make a change. I know what I am getting, and I am happy with it, so I will stick with it."

Female: "Price certainty does not bother me anyway. I know it is good gas, and it always has been."

Female: "I want the power for my small car. With a clean, pure gas, you get power."

Female: "I enjoy a station where they recognize me. I enjoy a smile on a friendly face and courteous service. At my favorite station, the owner knows what brand of cigarette I smoke and the gum I like."

TRUE BLUES: Primary Need Is Quality Service

Female: "I like my station. I can get in and out fast."

Male: "For me as a businessman, I want to zip in and fill it up and hit the road. If I could dream, it would be that someone would sneak into my garage and fill my car up with gas. Since that is not going to happen, I have to come in, fill it up, and get out without a hassle."

Male: "I have gotten to the point now that when I pull into a gas station when on the road traveling, I am really disappointed if I have to go inside and ask them to turn the pump on. Really, it is nice to just put your card in and pump the gas and get back on the road fast."

Male: "The car is it; I cannot afford to get stuck in traffic. I expect the car to perform when I want it to perform. When I step on the gas, I want to go. When I turn the key, I want it to start. Run and gun, that is me."

Male: "I like a new station with electronic pumps."

GENERATION F3: Primary Need Is Convenience Store

Female: "I pay with cash more than credit cards."

Male: "I don't like to pay at the pump since I don't have the credit rating for a card."

Female: "The convenience store is important to me. I will spend two to three dollars at a stop on cigarettes and a hot dog or sandwich and a cola drink."

Female: "I like a station that is convenient and has many locations."

Male: "Gassing up the vehicle is not a thrilling experience that you want to enjoy and prolong. Fast in and out is the key."

Male: "Convenient parking is important."

HOME BODIES: Primary Need Is Convenient Location

Female: "I don't drive much and like to go to the same station."

Female: "I look for a trusting and safe place to go to. I don't know much about cars."

Female: "Mobil gas, we are religious about it."

Female: "I just like my local station. I know I will get what I pay for."

Female: "I had a 4-runner at one time, and I was having trouble with the gas lid not opening, and the station attendant came out and opened it for me. It was really nice to have the help."

PRICE SHOPPERS: Primary Need Is Low Price

Male: "I watch for the station with the lowest price; why pay more?"

Male: "Gas is gas. Low price is the key."

Female: "I don't know one brand from another. I look for a good deal."

One example of the innovation process resulting from the educational seminars on strategic changes was the development of the Speedpass. A Speedpass is a small device carried on a key chain that, when waved in front of a photocell on a gasoline pump, identifies the consumer and charges the purchase to the appropriate credit or debit card. A manager in Mobil's technology section came up with the idea after learning of the importance of speed to customers.

Speedpass became a key differentiator in Mobil's marketing strategy. One of the great benefits of a fact-based needs segmentation study is the ability to communicate strategic information to the organization. The innovative concept of the Speedpass would not have been possible without this type of organizational communication and learning.

The strategy development team decided to monitor the execution of the new marketing program by using a "mystery shopper" program to measure the progress each month. These shoppers would purchase fuel and a snack at every Mobil station nationwide, and they were then asked to evaluate their buying experience on twenty-three specific criteria. Since Mobil sells through independent owners of gasoline stations, it included two additional metrics to its customer monitoring program: dealer profitability and dealer satisfaction. The goal was to motivate independent dealers to deliver a great buying experience that would retain and attract an increasing share of targeted customers.

LESSONS LEARNED—RECOGNIZING UNMET NEEDS

The Mobil Oil experience provided the student team with many valuable lessons. Among them, the belief that the organization's markets are drifting to "commoditization" may be a myth, with the real driver being the organization's failure to understand the "rules of the game" as determined by customer needs. The "rules of the game" determine winners and losers in competitive markets. Customer needs are diverse, and their importance in the purchase process varies by group of customers. Needs-based segmentation is a strategic tool to quantify these needs and provide management with the factual information to guide strategy formulation, leading to improved financial performance.

The central lesson learned was that the key lever for achieving a long-term competitive advantage at acceptable margins is found by first focusing on the structure of markets or "rules of the game" and then addressing organizational issues of competitive strategy and implementation. The Mobil Oil experience was a clear validation of this theme. The strategic challenge for contemporary managers is to objectively understand customer needs and then develop processes that efficiently create and deliver products and services that competitively respond to market requirements better than competitors' products and services.

THREE YEARS LATER

For three years, Mobil's marketing team worked to implement the new strategy. Some tactical programs were very successful, while others needed major revision. On balance, the new positioning strategy was a success in targeting consumers who were willing to pay price premiums for gasoline if they could buy at fast, friendly stations that were outfitted with excellent convenience stores.

Mobil targeted premium customer segments by offering:

- Immediate access to gasoline pumps, each equipped with a self-payment mechanism
- Safe, well-lit stations
- Clean restrooms
- Convenience stores stocked with fresh, high-quality merchandise
- Friendly employees
- Ancillary automotive products and services (car washes, oil changes, and minor repairs)
- Automotive products (oil, antifreeze, and wiper fluid)
- Common replacement parts (tires and wiper blades)

The new marketing strategy was designed to reconstruct Mobil from a centrally-controlled manufacturer of commodity products to a decentralized, customer-driven organization. Mobil's previous mass-market strategy, which tried to meet the diverse needs of all market segments, resulted in an undifferentiated, me-too approach to the market. This old strategy resulted in poor margin and profit performance.

The revenue growth strategy called for Mobil to target customer needs outside of its gasoline offerings. This included convenience store products and services, ancillary automotive services (car washes, oil changes, and minor repairs), automotive products (oil, antifreeze, and wiper fluid), and common replacement parts (tires and wiper blades). Also, the company would sell premium brands to customers, with the objective of increasing sales faster than the industry average.

In terms of productivity improvement, Mobil wanted to improve operating expenses per gallon sold—to the lowest level in the industry—and to extract more from existing assets, for example by reducing the downtime at its oil refineries and increasing their yields. Basically, Mobil improved operating processes through the use of supply chain management, asset utilization, and capacity management.

BOTTOM-LINE RESULTS

Mobil's corporate goal in changing from an unfocused, mass-market strategy to a multi-segment targeted market strategy was to increase Mobil's profit margins and revenue for gasoline and non-gasoline products. Mobil executed a remarkable turnaround in less than two years to become the industry's profit leader. This strategic move demonstrates that there is no such thing as a commodity business, only businesses that fail to recognize the strategic leverage in understanding the "rules of the game," using the needs-based segmentation approach.

Mobil reaped an extra $118 million a year in earnings from an additional two cents a gallon on its gas—a strategy that would not have been possible without the needs-based segmentation results. Cash flow was increased by more than $1 billion per year, resulting in Mobil becoming the industry's profit leader. Several years later, Mobil merged with Exxon to become Exxon/Mobil—one of the leading petroleum organizations in the world.

CLASS ENDS

Hewlett-Packard had been interviewing students during the semester and heard about the Market Research Procedures class and the role of needs-based segmentation in strategy formulation. The result was a Hewlett-Packard proposal to support me in conducting a needs-based research project on the growing business-to-business personal computer market. My study, which we will examine in the next chapter, would be conducted over the summer and made available as a Michigan Case Study (meaning the study was used in my business school classes in subsequent years). In need of a research assistant, I learned that Bob would be on campus that summer and later taking a job with McKinsey Consulting. He was a perfect fit for the project, and he accepted the position.

Chapter 5

Case Study Research Project: Computer Industry

T HE NEXT CHAPTER in the story of my marketing classes shows us another capability of the needs-based segmentation process: forecasting market successes and failures. By looking at which companies are identifying and responding to market needs, it can become possible to "pick winners and losers" to some extent—more effectively, in fact, than through the common approaches to stock picking discussed in Chapter 1. In 1991, my students and I were privileged to be asked to bring our skills to bear on a relatively new industry that would become a central part of the American economy and of most people's lives.

While working with the student team on the Mobil project, I received an office visit from representatives of Hewlett Packard Corporation (H-P). They were interviewing students for jobs and were interested in student comments regarding needs-based segmentation research. A new research grant had been approved by H-P to support academic research projects and case writing. The company encouraged me to submit a proposal for conducting a needs-based research study of the business-to-business personal computer market. Understanding this market was of special interest to H-P.

The project was quickly approved by H-P and was scheduled to start in June. In conversation with Bob, I learned that his position with McKinsey Consulting in Cleveland would not start until September. He accepted a summer research position on the H-P project, saying it would be a great experience for his new consulting career. To start the project, I had Bob assemble background information on the personal computer industry.[1] The resulting Michigan Case Study was used extensively over the years in my classes.

PERSONAL COMPUTER INDUSTRY (1945–1991)

Computer technology had emerged from World War II military research. For the next three decades, IBM and Digital Equipment Corporation (DEC) dominated the market with large mainframes and minicomputers. In 1977, Kenneth Olsen, founder of the minicomputer marketer DEC, stated, "There is no reason for any individual to have a computer in their home."[2] Despite this prediction, mail-order and retail kits appeared on the market, which allowed hobbyists to assemble computers at home.

The next few years brought increasingly integrated, preassembled personal computers to the market. In 1977, start-ups such as Apple Computer and others gained popularity with easy-to-use computers. Next, larger firms such as Hewlett-Packard, IBM, Sony, and Texas Instruments entered the market. DEC, given the wisdom of the founder, decided to watch an evolving market from the sidelines.

IBM Market Entry

In the past, firms like Hewlett-Packard, DEC, and IBM had viewed the personal computer market as being unimportant to the business segment. However, the increased capabilities of the personal computer made it a serious threat to these mainframe and mini-computer manufacturers. In 1981, IBM launched its first personal computer (PC), and in two years, it had 42% of the market.

IBM wisely recognized that its existing mainframe computing organization was not compatible with the new technology of the personal computer. Consequently, it created an autonomous organization in Florida, miles away from the East Coast head-quarters for mainframes. The new organization was free to pro-cure components from any source—to sell through its own channels—and develop a cost structure consistent with the com-petitive demands of the growing personal computer market.

The new IBM organization commissioned a start-up software firm, Microsoft, to write the operating system for the new PC. It adopted a microprocessor architecture designed by Intel and published the specifications for the PC system. The "open archi-tecture" strategy was designed to encourage software developers to write programs for the PC.[3] Apple Computer, with a "closed architecture" strategy, found its market share steadily slipping, to near 20% by 1982.

Compaq was formed in 1982 and had never been in the com-puter business. To enter the market, Compaq recruited retail dealers by granting them full access to its market, including large-volume corporate customers. By 1987, Compaq had witnessed substantial growth and profitability.

1991 was a period of competitive and technological change in the computer industry, with the growth of the personal computer in the business and consumer market. IBM's dominant market share had dropped, and an array of large and small competitors were fighting for competitive positions.

Market Characteristics

PC performance improved throughout the 1980s, and prices fell at a rapid pace. In addition, the range of software available for the personal computer expanded dramatically. Given this rapid market growth, other firms entered the market, offering "IBM clones." A low-priced portable clone was introduced to the market by Compaq in 1982, and Compaq rapidly became the fastest-growing firm in American history. In 1984, Dell Computer Corporation was incorporated.

The buyers of personal computers were usually grouped into four categories: (1) large and midsize business/government, (2) small businesses, (3) individual (home) buyers, and (4) educational institutions. In 1990, PC sales by category were: large and midsize business/government 46%, small business 24%, individual (home) 27%, and education 3%. The total market size in 1990 was $36 billion.

Large and midsize business/government organizations typically had large Management Information System (MIS) departments that purchased, maintained, and supported PCs from a centralized location. The MIS staff was highly trained and knowledgeable about PCs. Most large organizations had a diversity of PC brands, which required constant maintenance and support.

Small businesses typically had a limited MIS staff. The purchase of a PC involved issues of performance, reliability, price, and the support/service package. Given their limited knowledge of PCs, small businesses relied heavily on the recommendations of the distribution channel and PC magazines.

Individual buyers purchased PCs for home/office use. Most

buyers were first-time purchasers. It was believed that these buyers relied heavily on evaluations by Consumer Reports and PC magazines in selecting a brand. Apple was more successful in selling its PC to individuals and educational institutions than to business organizations.

Three distribution channels were involved in the sale of PCs: (1) retail outlets, (2) distributor/integrated resellers, and (3) direct distribution. The portion of sales through each channel was: retail 22%, distributor/integrated resellers 43%, and direct (catalog, phone, online, and sales representatives) 23%.

Dell Market Entry

The story of Michael Dell has been told many times. As a freshman at the University of Texas, he started a dorm room business by refurbishing IBM clones and selling them for as much as 40% less than comparable IBM machines. With revenue approaching $80,000 in 1984, Dell dropped out of college and founded the Dell Computer Corporation.

In 1985, Michael Dell shifted from refurbishing IBM clones to assembling the Dell-branded computer. Recognizing that most competitors distributed PCs through distributors, resellers, and retailers, Dell focused on taking orders directly from customers. The "Dell Direct Model" concentrated on dealing directly with the needs of large businesses and government institutions. For example, the Ford Motor Company had a contract with Dell for the exclusive purchase of Dell products and services.

State of the Personal Computer Industry by 1991

Seventy percent of computers sold in 1988 were mainframes, and the rest were servers. The market potential for mainframes, servers, and personal computers is presented in Figure 5.1 that follows. By 1990, the industry was dominated by personal computers, which accounted for 40% of sales in the United States. For medium and small businesses, the personal computer was bringing productivity improvements that previously had been the domain of large businesses.

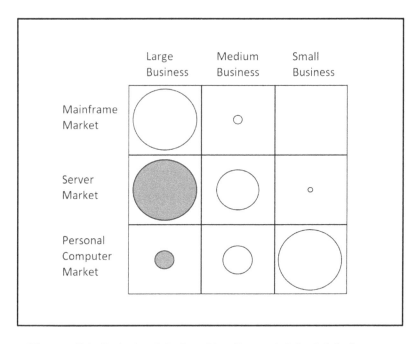

Figure 5.1. Relative Market Size Potential for Mainframes, Servers, and Personal Computers

In 1990, the personal computer industry experienced a tremendous shakeout of competitors due to market evolution combined with a recession. The personal computer industry growth rate was slowing and profit margins falling. Once an icon of technological innovation, the PC was now becoming a commodity product.

PERSONAL COMPUTER INDUSTRY KEY FINDINGS

Key findings from Bob's assembly of background information on the personal computer industry:

- The composition of business establishments in the US in 1991 indicated that 95% were small businesses.
- Almost all large businesses had PCs installed, whereas only half of small businesses had PCs installed.
- Of those businesses that did have PCs installed, small businesses had on average 5 PCs installed, whereas large businesses on average had 180 PCs installed.
- About 72% of large businesses intended to purchase PCs in the next 12 months, compared to 40% of small businesses.
- Of those businesses that intended to purchase personal computers, small businesses intended to purchase on average 4 PCs in the next 12 months, whereas large businesses intended to purchase on average 55 PCs in the next 12 months.
- The average price that businesses intended to pay per PC purchased in the next 12 months did not vary significantly with business size and was on average about $3,565.
- As business size increased, it became more likely that the selection of PCs would involve a central purchasing com-

mittee and that local branches would have less involvement in the purchase decision.

NEEDS-BASED SEGMENTATION STUDY

Once we had the background information from Bob, we were ready for the next step. The needs-based segmentation study was conducted by the same Detroit firm that did the Arbor Corporation study (discussed in Chapter 2). The same research process was followed, and the results were available in July.[4]

Table 5.1 presents the results of the 1991 personal computer segmentation study. Six focus groups were conducted with business managers, selected based on their roles in the purchase decision of personal computers. Participants were included from small, medium, and large businesses from around the United States. A list of over twenty primary needs was identified.

Segment Label	Primary Needs
Service/Support	Service support, ability to be run network, compatibility, expandable, system setup, basic training.
Cost Driven	Low cost, compatibility, immediate delivery, advice on hardware.
Technology Driven	Latest technology, service & support, network capability, an industry-leading brand name, superior graphics and speed, impressive looking.
Turn-Key System	Local service and support, sophisticated training, superior speed, networking capability.
Compatibility	Compatibility, low cost, ability to be networked, upgradeable, expandable.
Network Driven	Ability to be run network, superior speed, latest technology, local service & support, advice on hardware, impressive-looking.

Table 5.1. Buyer Needs in the PC Purchase Process

In 1991, a total of 409 business managers who were involved in the purchase of personal computers were contacted and agreed to be interviewed as part of the needs-based segmentation study. The sample of business managers was designed to be representative of personal computer sales by region of the country and by business size. The interview, which took approximately fifteen minutes, consisted of sixteen questions designed to quantify key personal computer marketing issues. The diverse set of needs identified in the focus groups was presented to the survey participants. The needs list was ranked from "most important" to "least important" in the purchase process for personal computers for the participants' organizations.

Cluster analysis identified six market segments, as shown in Figure 5.2 that follows. Figure 5.2 presents the market potential ($) of the six segments. Three segments accounted for three-fourths of the market potential: (1) Needs Service/Support—33%, (2) Cost Driven—21%, and (3) Needs Compatibility—20%.

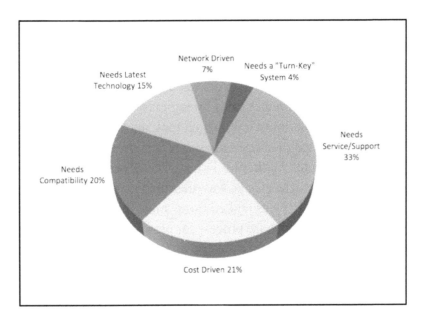

Figure 5.2. Market Segmentation Scheme Showing 1991 Business PC Market Potential (Total Market Potential = $23.4 Billion, 6.6 Million Units)

As shown in Table 5.2 that follows, the six market segments were evaluated as to the correlation with firmographic character-istics such as (1) Business Size, (2) Industry Classification, and (3) Geography. The highest correlation was with the "Needs Compatibility" segment. Large businesses have a greater need to purchase personal computers that are compatible with existing machines than small and medium businesses do. In addition, large businesses need less "Service/Support" and "Turn-Key Systems" than small and medium businesses. Large businesses had their own in-house computer support department to service their computer needs. Industry classification and geography showed a "weak to none" correlation with the six segments.

Cluster	1	5	4	6	3	2	
Need	Service	Compatibility	Turn Key	Network	Technology	Cost	Total

Business Size

	Service	Compatibility	Turn Key	Network	Technology	Cost	Total
Small	34%	20%	4%	5%	9%	28%	100%
Medium	30%	25%	5%	6%	9%	25%	100%
Large	19%	40%	0%	5%	10%	26%	100%

Industry Classification

	Service	Compatibility	Turn Key	Network	Technology	Cost	Total
Manfg	32%	25%	5%	2%	10%	26%	100%
Retail Dist.	36%	20%	3%	7%	7%	27%	100%
Wholesale	22%	30%	2%	6%	8%	32%	100%
Fin/Inst. Service	30%	32%	6%	4%	16%	12%	100%
School Govt	25%	21%	7%	6%	12%	29%	100%
Media	29%	28%	5%	2%	5%	31%	100%
Other	30%	31%	3%	5%	10%	21%	100%

Geography

	Service	Compatibility	Turn Key	Network	Technology	Cost	Total
East	32%	23%	5%	5%	11%	24%	100%
Mid	29%	26%	4%	7%	9%	25%	100%
West	30%	24%	6%	5%	10%	25%	100%

Table 5.2. Correlation of Business Size, Industry Classification, and Geography to Business PC Market Potential

SELECTING MARKET SEGMENTS

Figure 5.2 presented the six segments and the differences in buyer needs among segments. A competitive advantage is achieved by designing a superior differentiation strategy targeted to a segment.

For example, the "Needs Service/Support" segment would re-spond to a positioning strategy that provides these benefits: local service and support, ability to be/run a network, compatibility with existing systems, expandability, system setup, and basic training for employees. However, the "Cost Driven" (or "low price") segment would respond to a positioning strategy that offers a lower-priced computer that is compatible with existing systems, immediate delivery of the computer, and a hotline for advice on hardware issues.

The strategic challenge for the manufacturer is to determine which segment or segments to target. The market potential of the segments, the threat of competitive entry, and the cost structure to deliver benefits are important considerations. It may be difficult to design a differentiation strategy that meets the needs of more than one segment.

In Chapter 4 of this book, the Mobil Oil Company successful-ly targeted the non-price-sensitive segments with a multiple-benefit positioning strategy. This approach requires identifying important needs across segments that can be implemented by a single marketing program. Often, this is not possible, as in, for example, the case where low price is important to one segment and another segment expects superior benefits and a high brand reputation. The Southwest Airlines case study in Chapter 2 is an example of this strategic choice.

In formulating a competitive strategy, the manufacturer may have to lower the degree of differentiation targeted to a segment to gain greater market potential across multiple segments. Is it best to have a high share of a small market potential segment or a lower share of multiple segments where the degree of competitive differentiation is less? Strategy is about making trade-off choices, and this is clearly the case when designing a positioning strategy given a needs-based segmentation scheme. The bigger the total market potential, the greater the opportunity to focus on one or two segments with a multiple benefit strategy. The large and growing market potential in the personal computer market suggests that a niche strategy targeting a single segment is possible.

Previous research suggests there are three generic categories of needs in consumer, services, and business markets (as described in Chapter 1 of this book). There is a group of customers whose first priority is quality. They are willing to seek out goods and services that have superior quality and pay a premium price. We call this the "Benefit Segment." The "Needs Latest Technology" and "Network Driven" segments (shown in Figure 5.2) fit the benefit segment definition. In 1991, these two segments expected to pay the high price of $5,800 for a personal computer and desired an extensive list of benefits. A low price was less important to this group and may have been a signal to them that the quality of the good or service was low. These two segments represented 22% of the personal computer market potential.

The next segment is the "Price Segment." These are customers who view lower price as a key trade-off in the purchase process. The "Cost Driven" (or "low price") segment (shown in Figure 5.2) fits this definition with a short list of needs: compatibility, immediate delivery, advice on hardware, and a price point of $2,700. This segment represented 21% of the personal computer market potential.

The middle segment is the "Benefit/Price Segment." This is always a challenging segment since they want some degree of quality but at a reasonable price. The segments of "Needs Service/Support," "Needs Turn-Key System," and "Needs Compatibility" (shown in Figure 5.2) fit this definition. These three segments represented 57% of the market potential.

1991 MARKET SHARE AND CUSTOMER SATISFACTION

My study team's evaluation of competitive positions in 1991 started with reviewing the market shares of competitors and reviewing customer satisfaction scores. The 1991 market segmentation study provides information on both of these indexes for 1991. And a public data source provides a three-year history of market share trends from 1989 to 1991. By comparing the study estimates of market share with those of industry data collection firms, the validity of the market segmentation study can be evaluated. Table 5.3 that follows indicates that the market segmentation study and industry data sources show very similar estimates of competitors' market share.

	1989	1990	1991	1991 (Segment Results)*
IBM	16.9	16.1	14.1	18
Apple	10.7	10.9	13.7	12
Packard Bell	3.3	3.9	4.7	4
Compaq	4.4	4.5	4.1	4
AST/Tandy	1.7	1.8	2.5	5
Gateway	0.2	1.0	2.5	1
Dell	0.9	1.0	1.6	2
Other	61.9	60.8	56.6	52

* Market segmentation survey results vs. industry data.

Table 5.3. PC Market Shares 1989–1991 (Unit Share)[5]

Again, Table 5.3 presents the personal computer market shares in the United States as reported by a published source compared to the 1991 market segmentation study results. The biggest winner is "Other," with a market share of over 50%, as reported from both sources. The "Other" category included companies with very low share of markets (less than 1%).

The published source indicates that IBM's share of market had declined to 14% in 1991 and that the market share for "Other" had declined as well. Apple and Packard Bell had increased market shares. Compaq had a stable market share at 4%, while Dell and Gateway had increased their shares to around 2%.

Table 5.4 and Table 5.5 that follow present the market segmentation survey results regarding the degree of satisfaction customers experienced with their computers. The survey asked buyers to evaluate their computers on several positioning characteristics. The customer satisfaction profiles for competitors by market segments were presented. Large differences in customer satisfaction were observed among the positioning strategies of competitors.

(% Responding "Strongly Agree")

	IBM	Apple	P'bell	C'paq	AST	Tandy	G'way	Dell	Other	Total
Good service/support	31%	33%	32%	33%	35%	34%	36%	42%	21%	27%
Compatible with other PCs owned	85%	65%	70%	70%	71%	71%	63%	69%	52%	63%
Successful total system	70%	72%	67%	68%	67%	66%	67%	65%	66%	68%
Runs network successfully	85%	82%	69%	80%	59%	68%	66%	61%	48%	67%
Has latest technology	70%	85%	53%	72%	62%	52%	37%	36%	24%	46%
Had lowest cost for our needs	16%	22%	74%	71%	27%	66%	80%	83%	64%	49%

N=328

Table 5.4. Customer Satisfaction with PC Brand
Last Purchased

(6 = Very High, 1 = Very Low)

Apple	**5.2**
IBM	3.5
Compaq	2.0
AST	2.7
Gateway	2.6
Tandy	2.5
Packard Bell	2.4
Dell	2.3
Other	2.6
Total	3.0

N = 328

Table 5.5. Customer Loyalty to PC Brand Last Purchased

The following conclusions were drawn.

- The highest proportion of a PC brand last purchased was IBM, followed by Apple, Dell, Compaq, AST, and Tandy.
- The survey indicated that overall, respondents were unsatisfied with the service/support associated with their last PC purchase. Dell owners were the only exception.
- Respondents were only somewhat satisfied with the compatibility of the last PC they purchased with their other PCs. The most satisfied are IBM owners.
- Respondents who purchased their PC as part of a total system solution were only somewhat satisfied with the success of their total system, no matter what brand they own.
- Respondents who purchased their PC to run a network were mostly satisfied with its ability to run the network, no matter what brand they own.
- Overall, respondents were somewhat satisfied with the belief that their PC had the "latest technology" when they

purchased it. Apple owners were more satisfied than the rest.

- Dell owners were very satisfied that their PC had the lowest cost for their needs. Tandy and AST owners were somewhat satisfied, but IBM, Apple, and Compaq owners were extremely unsatisfied or disagreed with the idea that their PC had the lowest cost for their needs.
- The overall loyalty to the brand last purchased was somewhat low for all brands except Apple.

EVALUATION OF COMPETITIVE POSITIONING STRATEGIES

The Michigan Case Study that I used in my classes in the years following 1991 was based on the report to Hewlett-Packard. The following sections of this chapter, which involve students' evaluation of competitors' positioning strategies, were not included in the case study. The students' assignment was to evaluate the competitive positions of the key competitors and to forecast winners and losers. The positioning analyses and forecasts presented in the following sections represent the typical student reports.

Students were reminded that the "rules of the game" in a market are determined by customer wants and needs. When a competitor plays by the rules, the customer rewards the competitor with revenue. The key to developing a competitive advantage is to understand and play by the rules. The key to a successful positioning strategy is to understand and play by the rules for a target segment. How well did the various competitors do by this criterion? Let's find out by examining them individually in the subsections that follow.

The "Other" Category

The large "Other" category of competitors, which (as shown in Table 5.3) had the largest market share, clearly was not playing by the rules. Table 5.4 shows that they had low satisfaction scores on all positioning dimensions except for "Had lowest cost." The lowest satisfaction score was on the "Good service/support" question. Figure 5.1, Relative Market Size Potential, indicated that the largest market potential for personal computers was with small businesses. And Table 5.2 indicated that a significant component of the "Needs Good Service/Support" segment included small and medium businesses.

The small market share companies combined into the "Other" category had a marketing strategy of entering the growing PC market with a weak positioning strategy based on low price. They distributed their computers through retail stores with little attention to the market needs for service and support. The poor customer satisfaction evaluations would suggest continued decline in share of market for these small share competitors.

Table 5.4 indicates that Packard Bell, AST, Tandy, Gateway, and Dell were also evaluated as "Had lowest cost for our needs." The lower price strategy of these competitors also led to lower brand loyalty and equity, as shown in Table 5.5. However, Table 5.4 indicates that these five higher-market share competitors had stronger positioning strategies than those in the "Other" category, especially on the "Good service/support" question. The combined unit sale market share for all of the low-price competitors was 68% in 1991, as reported in Table 5.3. The initial success of these competitors can be found in the price sensitivity of a large segment of the market as well as in customers' lack of experience with personal computers due to the early stages of the market's evolution. **The 1991 market segmentation study would fore-**

cast that future years should see a significant shakeout of these small "Other" category competitors and a consolidation of the larger share players.

IBM Computer

In 1991, IBM was still the market leader in the PC market, but with slowing sales, growing competition, and evolving market conditions. Falling prices of PC components and standardization on the Windows operating system and Intel processor technology facilitated mass production of PCs. Users were becoming more knowledgeable about PC installation, which facilitated the migration toward direct distribution by the adoption of standard software products like Microsoft applications. Because of the technological and market changes, many PC users no longer required the technical know-how of the indirect channel during the buying process.

Table 5.4 indicates that IBM had a strong competitive positioning but that its positioning was similar to Compaq. IBM brand loyalty/equity was second in the industry, only surpassed by Apple, as shown in Table 5.5. IBM was a strong competitor in the large segments shown in Figure 5.2 of "Needs Service/Support" and "Needs Compatibility." But the "Cost Driven" segment was a problem. Remember, IBM was the leader in mainframes with large businesses. However, large businesses are an important component of the "Cost Driven" segment, which has a different set of need priorities than other segments (see Table 5.1, Buyer Needs).

IBM's marketing strategy for the "Needs Service/Support" and "Needs Compatibility" segments (of Figure 5.2) was to maintain a strong distributor/reseller and retail store program which could supply needed service and support, which were important to these segments. However, competitors like Compaq were doing the same, and price competition was aggressive. In addition, Dell was aggressively competing in the "Cost driven" segment with a well-positioned marketing program of direct sale and distribution to large businesses.

The result for IBM was declining market share and poor profit performance. This result was compounded by a serious strategic error made in 1987 from which IBM was still trying to recover. Failing to recognize the pervasive need of the market segment for "Needs Compatibility," IBM announced new internal computer architecture called MCA-Micro Channel Architecture. This new architecture changed the size and electrical configuration of the slots in a PC that were used for add-on boards. The result was that computers using MCA did not permit the use of third-party add-on boards such as modems or expanded memory. Eight PC manufacturers, under the leadership of Compaq, announced the Extended Industry Standard Architecture (EISA) that was compatible with existing industry standards.

We have now seen that through the remainder of the 1990s, IBM's competitive position would continue to decline. The company decided to streamline its hardware operations with divestitures, and it used acquisitions to augment its software and service businesses. It edged itself out of the commodity hardware business by selling its PC manufacturing facilities to Sanmina-SCI Corp. and its hard drive unit to Hitachi, Ltd. in 2002. **The 1991 needs-based segmentation study had forecast difficult years ahead for the IBM personal computer business.**

Dell Computer

Dell Computer was one of the low-priced competitors that found growing success in the personal computer market. Many books, articles, and case studies have been devoted to telling the Dell story. Let's evaluate the results of the 1991 needs-based segmentation study and forecast what lies ahead for Dell.

As we have seen previously, Dell's market share had been increasing, so it must have been doing something right. Table 5.4 indicates that customers gave Dell the highest satisfaction score of all competitors on "Had lowest cost for our needs" and "Good service/support." Dell also had the next to lowest satisfaction score on "Has latest technology," however, the "Needs Latest Technology" was a small segment of the market (as shown in Figure 5.2) and most likely not a target market of interest to Dell.

Dell's positioning strategy was very competitive in the "Cost Driven" and "Needs Compatibility" segments (of Figure 5.2). Remember, there was an array of competitors all competing for these customers. Let's review the type of value proposition that appeals to these two segments. A strong value proposition would be one that addresses segment needs better than the competition does. Table 5.1 identified the needs of these two segments. A strong value proposition would directly address the following needs:

- Low Cost—important to both segments
- Compatibility—important to both segments
- Immediate Delivery—important to "Cost Driven" segment
- Advice on Hardware—important to "Cost Driven" segment
- Ability to be networked, upgradeable, and expandable— important to "Compatibility" segment

Table 5.2 indicated that the buyer profile for the "Needs Compatibility" segment was primarily large businesses. Large businesses needed to purchase personal computers that were compatible with existing machines to a higher degree than small and medium businesses did. In addition, large businesses needed less "Service and Support" and "Turn-Key Systems" than small and medium businesses. Large businesses had their own technical staff who could service and support the firms' large computer base.

Michael Dell started his business selling refurbished IBM clones to large businesses at 40% less than comparable IBM machines. This initial customer contact provided information as to the important needs of large businesses. Dell took orders directly from large customers and provided immediate delivery by shipping computers directly to them via the mail. Remember, large businesses had their own technical staff who could install and service the Dell computer.

Software was not an issue either for large businesses, which could install their own software on the Dell computer if needed. However, large buyers did want to have a "hotline" to Dell so that any technical issues with the computers could be resolved quickly. These issues could relate to compatibility problems in running the network or upgrading existing computers. Maintaining a technical staff is expensive, and large businesses that have invested in doing so don't want to buy from a computer company that must charge higher prices to cover its own costs for service and support, relevant to other segments of the market who are willing to pay for it.

The 1991 market segmentation study indicated that Dell had a strong positioning strategy compared to competitors. **The needs-based segmentation study was able to forecast that Dell's market share would continue to grow in the years ahead. This was borne out, as IBM and "Other" competitors would continue to lose market share to Dell.**

Gateway 2000

Gateway 2000 was the second-largest direct marketer of personal computers, trailing only Dell. Like Dell, Gateway took orders from customers, produced an IBM clone to specifications, loaded software, and shipped PCs directly to the customer. The target customer was the sophisticated home and small business user. Table 5.4 indicates that Gateway's competitive positioning was very similar to Dell's, both offering a very low price. The main difference was Dell's focus on large- and medium-sized businesses, while Gateway targeted the small business market.

Table 5.2 indicated that the small business market required a higher degree of service and support than larger businesses. Gateway provided this service and support by maintaining a sales force, which provided extensive telephone and Web-based technical support, and by contracting with third parties for on-site technical service. This strategy fit well with the needs of small businesses in the "Cost Driven" and "Needs Compatibility" segments (of Figure 5.2): those who desired low-cost, compatibility, immediate delivery, advice on hardware, and expandability. **The 1991 needs-based segmentation study would forecast continued share growth for Gateway, given its repositioning to the small business customer.**

Hindsight shows that Gateway grew at an annual rate of 40% from 1991 to 1996 and briefly surpassed Dell in sales for 1994. However, a series of poor strategic decisions resulted in slower growth and declining profits thereafter. In 1997, Gateway acquired Advanced Logic Research with the objective of expanding into the growing server market of medium and large businesses. At the same time, Gateway set up Gateway Major Accounts, Inc., a company within the company, to service large corporate, government, and educational customers. This strategic misstep put

Gateway in direct competition with Dell and Compaq. In 1998, Gateway cut back marketing programs directed to large businesses and refocused its strategy on small businesses.

Compaq Computer

Compaq was founded in 1982. It had never been in the computer business and had no sales force of its own. To enter the market, Compaq recruited retail dealers by promising them full control of the market, including large-volume corporate accounts. Over the next several years, Compaq witnessed substantial growth, selling PCs through independent, full-service computer specialty dealers. Table 5.4 shows Compaq's competitive positioning to be above the industry average on all dimensions except "Had lowest cost for our needs." Compaq's strong positioning strategy allowed it to be aggressive in pricing its computers, resulting in above-industry margins and profits.

The large base of IBM compatibles made it lucrative for the development of software programs written for the MS-DOS operating system developed by the Microsoft Corporation. This led to an explosion in application software available in the IBM-PC/MS-DOS environment. IBM's market share continued to drop over the years, while Compaq, Packard Bell, and Gateway grew. Retail chains like BusinessLand and ComputerLand provided the service and support important to small and medium businesses, which represented a very large component of the personal computer market potential.

It is important to recognize that by 1991, the hardware part of the personal computer was becoming a commodity business. Software applications and service and support were becoming major issues in the purchase process along with lower prices, especially among small and medium-sized businesses. In Figure

5.2, the three segments of "Needs Service/Support," "Cost Driven," and "Needs Compatibility" represent nearly 75% of the market potential. **The 1991 needs-based segmentation study would forecast growing market share for Compaq, given its solid competitive positioning.**

Apple Computer

Apple was an early entrant to the personal computer market and was the clear technology leader. It offered a unique operating system with an intuitive and easy Graphical User Interface (GUI) that enabled applications to be driven by a simple point-and-click menu system. This ease of use attracted many first-time users in the consumer and educational market.

Apple's market share grew in 1991 to near that of IBM (see Table 5.3). Table 5.4 indicates that Apple's competitive positioning was very strong, especially on the question "Has latest technology." Apple's target was, and still is, the "Needs Latest Technology" segment of Figure 5.2 (with "Technology Driven" customers' needs defined in Table 5.1), and it has dominated competitors in this segment with a superior marketing program and a higher price point. In addition to the latest technology, Apple's customers needed superior service and support, network capability, a leading brand name, and impressive-looking and superior graphics/speed.

Apple's strong positioning to the "Needs Latest Technology" segment resulted in superior brand equity in that segment compared to other PC manufacturers (see Table 5.4). And, like Compaq, Apple distributed through retail chains like BusinessLand and ComputerLand, which provided the service and support important to small and medium businesses. But Apple's market share declined dramatically for the next six years. What can we learn from the needs-based segmentation study that would forecast this decline?

Apple's 1991 competitive positioning was a strong, focused strategy positioned in the smaller "Needs Latest Technology" segment. The competitive challenge ahead of Apple was to expand its market share to other market segments. Such expansion would require addressing the common need of "compatibility" present in all the remaining segments. Apple's strategic Achilles' heel, preventing it from implementing a multiple segment strategy, was its unique operating system, which was not compatible with the IBM "open" architecture system required by other segments.

The 1991 needs-based segmentation study would forecast continued market share gain for Apple if it made a strategic change to an "open" architecture system. If not, failure to recognize that the "rules of the game" do not allow Apple to expand its strategic scope could lead to ill-advised investments and a resulting market share decline. Given the organizational culture at Apple, the chance of this change was slim, and most likely, limited share growth seemed to be ahead for Apple. The company's later success has come from developing innovative new products for its current market, from the iPod to the Tablet to the iPhone.

MICHIGAN CASE STUDY

The case study that I used in my classes in the years following 1991 (and was based on the 1991 needs-based segmentation study report to Hewlett-Packard) addressed two issues. First, can a useful needs-based segmentation study be conducted early in the innovation cycle of a disruptive technology? And second, given the "rules of the game," can a needs-based segmentation study forecast the evolution of competitive positions? Students were challenged to discuss this and other issues from the case study.

During the student discussion, an important issue was raised regarding the stability of the needs-based segmentation results over time. If the needs of businesses change quickly, the accuracy of the competitive position forecast would be limited to the short-run. In response, I indicated that research on consumer market needs suggests stability over time. However, little research is reported on business-to-business needs.

To stimulate the discussion, I asked the question, "If the technology of a competitor changed, would this impact segmentation results?" This could easily impact the value proposition of a competitor. Several students said yes and cited Apple as an example. If Apple had initially chosen to have an open architecture, the need for compatibility would be less of an issue. Consequently, Apple's future competitive position would be significantly improved given its positioning strength in other needs such as "latest technology" and "brand image." The class ended with the conclusion that only time will determine the stability issue for the computer needs-based segmentation study.

The final class of the semester was always difficult for me. You get to know students personally, and seeing them off to their new lives and careers is exciting. Hopefully, what they have learned in the two years of their MBA program will serve them well. Regarding this book's theme of the importance of needs-based segmentation in forecasting business success, I would suggest that looking ahead through the eyes of the customer may be the secret to forecasting rather than the traditional use of historical records. If this is the case, stock picking may see a new day. The epilogue that follows has an interesting follow-up to this perspective.

Epilogue

Making Millions: Class of 1984 Twenty-Year Reunion

Y EARS AFTER HAVING Bob in my class, there was a real surprise in store for me. It turned out that the lessons my students learned about using segmentation studies to forecast the relative success of companies had more than one application.

When the MBA class of 1989 held its twenty-year class reunion at the Ross School of Business, it was great for me to see the students and their families. Fortunately, name tags helped my twenty-year-old memory recognize students. One student I found easy to remember was Bob Swanson. After working for McKinsey, he had moved on to become Director of Marketing for a leading US company. I was very surprised to find out that he had retired to a beach city in California. I commented that the corporate life appeared to be very profitable. He laughed and said the real profits came from his MBA experience.

Bob explained that, upon leaving the Ross School of Business for McKinsey, the H-P personal computer research project had left him with a great idea. Was it possible that the secret to forecasting future business success was to be found in a needs-based segmentation study? He recognized that financial information was only a record of the past and provided limited insight into the future success of an organization. The strategic issue was how do you look ahead and forecast winners and losers in a competitive market? Needs-based segmentation was the secret answer, in that management can see oncoming traffic and curves in the road with quantitative numbers rather than speculation based on past experiences.

Bob had learned that the "rules of the game" were defined by customer needs and wants. Competitors who play by the rules are rewarded by customers, with revenue. The critical insight is that customers can have very different needs and wants. Such differences form the basis for market segments. A needs-based segmentation procedure can quantify these differences and provide valuable strategic insight for an organization. The needs-based segmentation study of the personal computer market was Bob's opportunity to put what he had learned in the Michigan MBA to the test.

FORECASTING THE FUTURE

Bob explained that, upon completion of the Personal Computer study, it was clear to him who the winners and losers would be over the years. In 1991, Apple had the leading market share with very high customer satisfaction scores, but its share of market was declining as the use of PCs became widespread in a wide range of business settings. The needs-based segmentation study suggested that Apple would be a strong player in a smaller niche segment of the market.

It would be easy to argue that Apple would be a winner in the future if its leadership operated a major change in their software strategy. However, Apple was not playing by the "rules of the game" in the larger, business-oriented segments of the market and most likely would not change its positioning strategy. The need for compatibility was the primary benefit requirement in the growing personal computer market. Consequently, Apple did not appear at the time to be a great stock purchase.

In contrast, the needs-based segmentation study forecasted that Compaq, Gateway, and Dell were in strong competitive positions for share growth. At this point, it was time for Bob to put money behind his beliefs. In 1992, Bob bought $7,000 in stock with these three companies. He bet heavily on Dell, given its business model and its focus on large and medium businesses. Dell's dramatic surge in price a year later supported Bob's beliefs, and he bought $500,000 more in stock.

Dell's stock split seven times, and by 1999, the company had a market share of 14%. Compaq moved to a 16% share and Gateway to 8%. At that point, Bob decided to retire to California with several million in the bank. He said again that it was thanks to that Michigan MBA and that he can say "GO BLUE" with pride. Bob ended his story by suggesting I revise my course notes that suggest you can't beat the average of the stock market. The secret is a quantitative needs-based segmentation study which forecasts future competitive winners and losers. (Dell's substantial growth in profits and stock price are shown in the following figure.)

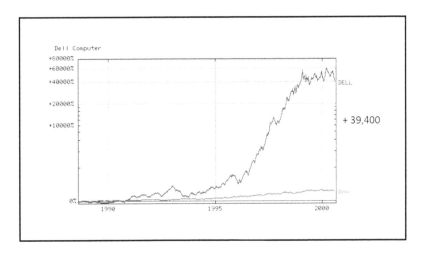

Figure Epilogue 1. Stock Chart: Dell Computer Shareholder Wealth Versus the Dow Average (to 2000)

I never told this story behind Bob's retirement to my wife since she believes I am a smart business professor. I am sharing it with you in the hopes that you, too, can make millions. But please keep the story from my wife!

From the Publisher

Thank You from the Publisher

Van Rye Publishing, LLC ("VRP") sincerely thanks you for your interest in and purchase of this book.

VRP hopes you will please consider taking a moment to help other readers like you by leaving a rating or review of this book at your favorite online book retailer. Depending on the retailer, you can do so by flipping past the last page of your e-book (to the rating and review page) or by visiting the book's product page (and locating the button for leaving a rating or review).

Thank you!

Resources from the Publisher

Van Rye Publishing, LLC ("VRP") offers the following resources to readers and to writers.

For *readers* who enjoyed this book or found it useful, please consider receiving updates from VRP about new and discounted books like this one. You can do so by following VRP on Facebook (at www.facebook.com/vanryepub) or Twitter (at www.

twitter.com/vanryepub).

For *writers* who enjoyed this book or found it useful, please consider having VRP edit, format, or fully publish your own book manuscript. You can find out more and submit your manuscript at VRP's website (at www.vanryepublishing.com).

Thank you again!

Appendix A

Class Note: Strategic Concepts and Processes in Business Strategy

THIS CLASS NOTE reviews the strategic concepts and processes that underlie contemporary business strategy. First will be discussed the evolution of competitive dynamics in the United States. Next, a "Value/Cost" framework is presented and evaluates the strategic positioning of competitors in an industry. This framework can be used in class to evaluate the competitive positions and strategic moves of firms in the industry being studied. A key component of this framework is the concept of needs-based market segmentation, which is presented in another class note (in Appendix B of this book). The goal is to position needs-based segmentation in the broader strategic processes of an organization. Needs-based segmentation is a key ingredient in the organizational challenge of creating and maintaining a sustainable competitive advantage (SCA).

EVALUATING COMPETITIVE POSITIONS

Given the competitive environment of an industry, economists have focused attention on the question: Why do some competitors outperform other competitors over an extended period of time? This persistence of profitability is referred to as a "sustainable competitive advantage." Sustainable competitive advantage (SCA) refers to decisions by the organization that leverage marketing mix differentiation and/or cost structures relative to competition over a strategically significant time period. These two levers for sustainable financial growth can be viewed as processes to drive both: (1) revenue growth and (2) productivity improvement.

As further detailed in Figure A.1 that follows, revenue growth can be achieved in two ways, in either existing markets or new ones:

- Increase the value of existing products and services
- Develop new products

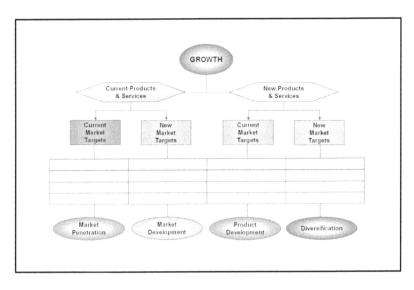

Figure A.1. Revenue Growth Alternatives

The productivity strategy also has two parts:

- Improve the organization's cost structure by reducing direct and indirect expenses
- Use assets more efficiently by reducing the working and fixed capital needed to support a given level of business[1]

It is important to recognize how the financial benefits from these two components (revenue growth vs. productivity improvement) differ in the time required to produce results. Short-term benefits typically come from increased operational efficiencies and process improvements. The popularity of books on Japanese management, quality management, turnaround management, and downsizing reflects management's desire for fast solutions to financial problems. However, business processes that are fast and easy to implement have short-lived competitive effects. They are easily matched by competitors, and any differential advantage is rapidly neutralized. Such actions are a necessary but not sufficient process in the search to gain a sustainable competitive advantage.

Revenue growth resulting from improvements in the value consumers receive from changes to existing products/services and from innovations with new products for existing and new customers requires more time. The business processes that support such improvements require a management culture that is long-run oriented and customer-focused. Needs-based segmentation outlines the "rules of the game" that guide the development of critical business processes to successfully implement a revenue growth strategy. Remember, improved cash flow only comes from revenue growth, not productivity improvement.

Finally, to develop and maintain an organizational culture that can achieve a sustainable competitive advantage, senior executives must balance the organizational trade-offs required to implement successful revenue growth and productivity processes. Too often, the organizational culture favors the short-run productivity lever. In addition, the challenges and frustrations of improving productivity can drive out the long-run process needed for revenue growth.

Bob Lutz, a former executive at Chrysler and General Motors, states:

> What does it take to inspire people and defeat a bean-counting corporate bureaucracy? There is little or no competitive advantage to be gained by trying even harder in procurement, manufacturing, or wholesale. Where the real work of making a car company successful suddenly turns complex, and where the winners are separated from the losers, is in the long-cycle product development process, where short-term day-to-day metrics and the tabulation of results are meaningless. Too often, we hear how much can be cut before the customer will start complaining. It will be death by a thousand small cuts because anytime the company loses the focus of providing the very best it can, delighting the eye, ear, butt, and wallet of the customer more than the competitors do, the inevitable decline sets in.[2]

Marketing Mix Differentiation

Choices regarding the components of the marketing program are referred to as the "marketing mix." The marketing mix is composed of decisions regarding (1) product/service specifications, (2) distribution, (3) promotion, and (4) pricing.

The nature and quality level of the products and services involves coordination with product design, manufacturing, purchasing, and human resource management. The distribution of the product and/or service involves coordination with physical distribution, wholesalers/retailers, and warranty and service contracts. Promotion to the customer and distribution channel involves coordination with advertising agencies, public relations firms, and trade and customer promotion departments. Finally, the bundle of benefits must be priced for the marketplace. Pricing significantly impacts trade and consumer demand for the offering as well as the margin structures available for profit objectives. The term "positioning" refers to this specialization of either the marketing program or the specialization of a single component, i.e., advertising positioning. A marketing program targeted to meet the important needs of a market segment will increase the level of marketing mix differentiation.

An organization's marketing program is the primary face of differentiation in the marketplace. Consumers evaluate the organization based on how well the marketing program serves customer needs. The buyer determines the degree of differentiation present in the marketing program by comparing it to competitors' marketing programs. The decision to buy is based on the highest perceived "value" offered in the marketplace. The highest value is not necessarily the lowest price offered. Rather, value is the perceived utility derived from the benefits offered (product/service policy, placement policy, and promotion policy) compared to the price. The customer perceives a benefit when a part of the marketing program satisfies an important buyer need.

Buyer needs can take many forms: functional characteristics (speed, energy consumption, etc.); economy (price, operating cost, etc.); and emotional/psychological factors (risk, prestige, fashion, etc.). A competitor increases the value of a marketing program by lowering the price and/or increasing the benefits offered. Differentiation increases for a competitor as the value of the marketing program increases. Consequently, higher differentiation can be achieved by improving benefits and/or lower prices.

Cost Structure Differentiation

Cost structure refers to all the variable and fixed costs that an organization incurs to produce and maintain its marketing program. A sustainable competitive advantage could come from an array of cost sources. The sources of cost advantage include: (1) economies of scale, (2) learning effects, (3) shared activities, (4) location, and (5) technology.

The largest cost centers in an organization relate to marketing and manufacturing expenditures. The sources of cost advantages typically are found in one or both of these areas. The challenge in this type of cost analysis is to understand the linkage among cost activities and the high leverage differentiation components of the marketing program. This type of analysis is growing in strategic importance and is referred to as "value engineering" and "benefit–cost analysis."

VALUE/COST DIFFERENTIATION

Let us return to the earlier question: Why do some competitors outperform other competitors over an extended period of time? One explanation is that competitors gain sustainable advantages through their marketing program differentiation and/or cost structure differentiation. Figure A.2 presents a framework for profiling strategic zones in the matrix of these two differentiation dimensions. The strategic zones are: (1) Benefit Leadership, (2) Cost Leadership, (3) Combination Leadership, and (4) Black Hole.

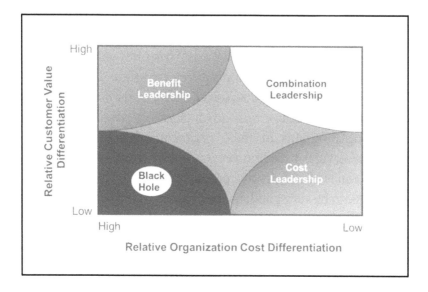

Figure A.2. Value/Cost Matrix

1. Benefit Leadership

Organizations with high marketing mix differentiation relative to competitors but with high relative cost structures are referred to as Benefit Leaders. Typically, organizations with this strategic positioning have used their higher cost structure to produce superior and innovative benefits in the marketplace. Their competitive advantage is sustained by continual product/service innovation. Examples of organizations in this strategic zone might include Porsche, Rolex watches, and Wynn resorts.

Benefit Leadership Characteristics:

- Ability to confer unique benefit(s) to the market
- Benefits must be important to an economically viable market segment (typically a niche segment)
- Benefits must be defendable or not easily copied
- Focus on margin-gain objective

2. Cost Leadership

Organizations with low relative cost structures and low relative marketing mix differentiation are referred to as Cost Leaders. These organizations have achieved lower costs by using one or more of the sources of cost advantages discussed earlier. The marketing programs of these organizations typically include products/services based on reverse engineering, which are "me too" or copies of competitive products. While the quality of these products can be very good, the products do not offer leading-edge innovation or possess the brand equity of Benefit Leaders. Examples of organizations in this strategic zone include manufacturers of store-branded jeans, Schwinn bicycles, low-budget motels, and Dollar stores.

Cost Leadership Characteristics:

- "Acceptable Benefits" at low prices
- Multi-segment or mass-market strategy
- Significant and sustainable cost advantages
- Focus on volume/share-gain objective

3. Combination Leadership

Organizations with high marketing mix differentiation and low cost structures are referred to as Combination Leaders. Organizations that are able to achieve this strategic zone have the best of both marketing mix differentiation and low cost structures. This strategic zone is difficult to achieve and requires excellence on many dimensions.

These organizations are typically leaders in their industry in terms of profitability. Academics and consultants study such organizations to identify the best practices that characterize their competitive advantage. These organizations typically use a focused market segmentation strategy that provides superior benefits to important customer needs. The organizational culture is one that can balance the trade-off between long-run revenue gain processes and the shorter-term productivity gains. The introduction of Lexus by Toyota is an example of a combination leadership strategy. Swatch watch is another example of a combination leadership strategy.

Combination Leadership Characteristics:

- Clear understanding of target market segment needs and importance
- Organizational processes that can manage the trade-off among customer value differentiation and organizational cost structures

4. Black Hole

Organizations with low marketing mix differentiation and high cost structures are typically in, or headed toward, serious financial trouble. A dynamic competitive landscape can drive firms toward the black hole. Competitive positioning is like an automobile race; failure to keep up with the competition will change your relative position in the race and drive the firm into the black hole. Firms moving toward the black hole are typically candidates for leadership change and turnaround management processes. The strategic challenge is to balance the short-term and long-term actions that will reposition the organization toward a healthy competitive position. General Motors, Braniff Airlines, and Sears are painful examples of this situation.

Stuck-in-the-Middle

A danger zone in the Value/Cost Matrix is being positioned in the middle. Here, competitors have moderate marketing mix differentiation and average cost structures. This zone characterizes competitors in many industries. These competitors are typically late entrants to a market with a "me-too" or "copy" strategy. They gain volume due to the expansion of the total market size and produce average or below-average profits. When the industry slows, these competitors are shakeout candidates or are merged with competitors in stronger strategic zones.

The Value/Cost Matrix and Strategic Choices

Strategy implies the movement of an organization from its present position in the Value/Cost Matrix to a more desirable location. Strategic change implies organizational risk in moving to a new position. Fact-based information provided by a needs-based segmentation study can facilitate the decision-making process by reducing the uncertainty surrounding strategic choices.

CONCLUSION

This class note presented key strategic concepts and processes that set the stage for focusing on industry examples of needs-based segmentation studies. The author believes that organizations that invest time and resources into conducting such studies will achieve an improved competitive position for their businesses. We end with the following list of best practices as determined by a leading consulting firm (source: Accenture Consulting).

- Fact-based discipline supporting all decision-making with a long-term profit focus
- Needs-based segmentation used to support strategic decisions
- Deliberate targeting and value proposition development
- Rigorous development of a strategic and tactical planning

process
- Coordination of Marketing, Sales, and Service; inclusive/leadership of all functions and activities that touch the customer and drive customers' experiences
- Rigorous performance measurement, analysis, planning, and feedback
- Marketing staffed with world-class talent
- Extensive management time devoted to understanding customers/consumers

Appendix B

Class Note: Methodology for Conducting a Needs-Based Segmentation Study

GETTING STARTED

The most sophisticated needs-based segmentation study is doomed to failure if managers do not support and believe in the information provided. In my experience, it is imperative to form an internal working team composed of key managers in marketing, manufacturing, product development, and sales. The active involvement of each of these user groups in the needs-based segmentation process assures understanding of and comfort with the information.

Organizations that invest in establishing common understanding and ownership among these critical parties can avoid subsequent criticism that the findings are flawed or not useful. Participation in the research process encourages managers to become champions of the approach with their colleagues in their functional units. In addition, these same managers play an important role in educating senior management about the segmentation project, its applications, and its benefits.

Step 1: Exploratory Research Phase

The foundation of segmentation research relies on the development of a comprehensive and accurate list of customer needs. This list of needs must reflect the criteria used by customers in the purchase decision process for the current or potential market. A skilled focus group moderator or face-to-face interviewer is required to accurately identify and refine the list of needs. This is a person who can listen to and interpret the language of the consumer without the bias of the language of the organization in the background.

I wish to emphasize again that this phase is the backbone of the segmentation study. The "garbage in, garbage out" principle directly applies here. Remember, customer needs are not easily discovered. It takes a skilled eye and a tested professional interviewer to develop a valid list of customer needs.

The following steps present the procedures used by the author in conducting this exploratory qualitative research phase.

1. Develop a contact list of current or potential customers in the market of interest. If such a list is not available, a telephone interviewing process can be used to screen for current or potential customers who can come to a focus group session or face-to-face interview.

2. Prepare interviewing materials. Documents must be developed, such as a letter of introduction, a screening questionnaire, topic guides, and possibly a brief structured questionnaire to explore and test issues.

3. Employ knowledgeable and skilled interviewers. There is a trick regarding the background of the interviewer. I have found that the interviewer should be one who thoroughly understands the product/service market situation. However, the interviewer's role is to portray a position of an "outsider" to the interviewee(s). This allows the interviewer to ask "naïve" questions that require the interviewees to explain in depth their knowledge of the issue.

4. Place special importance on the analysis of the results. If focus groups are involved, the session must be audiotaped and preferably videotaped. Hours will be required to review the tapes and analyze the content of the focus group sessions. Typically, four to eight focus group sessions will be required to adequately understand the needs of the market under study. A written report of the results must clearly identify the key needs of the market.

Step 2: Conclusive Research Phase

The second phase requires a survey across a scientifically drawn sample of consumers or organizations within the market of interest. This survey research phase involves the development and administration of a structured series of questions designed to test and validate the customer's needs-based decision process. The primary objective of the survey is to identify needs-based segments, estimate the size of the segments, and profile the characteristics of the segments. For business-to-consumer (B2C) markets, profiling could include such descriptors as age, sex, income, and geography. For business-to-business (B2B) markets, descriptors might include firm size and Standard Industrial Classification (SIC) code.

In summary, this phase of research has three objectives:

1. Identification of key segments and sub-segments of needs in a market
2. Determination of the size of market segments
3. Specification of the relevant differences in the characteris-

tics of the segments (e.g., demographics or firmographics)

The following steps present the procedures used by the author in conducting this conclusive qualitative research phase.

1. Determine the type of information required and develop a questionnaire to collect this information. The development process benefits from a "mocking up" of potential answers to the questions. An inspection of this hypothetical data can determine if the questions satisfy research objectives. While this exercise can detect gaps between objectives and potential data to be collected, it can also be used to identify redundant information.

2. Acquire a list of current or potential customers from which a probability sample can be drawn. Our experience suggests that sample size should not be determined entirely by statistical calculations. It is important that the sample size be large enough to be credible to management and to allow adequate cross-tabulations and segment size determinations. Typically, these requirements dictate that the sample size be larger than that required for statistical purposes.

3. Pilot-test the questionnaire with customers. The results of this testing will facilitate question revision and ensure that the flow of the questions makes sense to both interviewer and interviewee.

4. Select the data collection method. The most efficient and effective data collection method is the telephone interview for consumer and service markets. B2B research may require the use of the telephone to screen respondents and obtain cooperation in completing a mail questionnaire or a face-to-face interview.

5. Quality control procedures are critical during the data collection period. It is important to select a reputable and experienced marketing research firm that follows proper quality control procedures. The areas of concern are as follow:

- Extensive pretesting of the screening questionnaire
- Training and supervision of interviewers
- Monitoring or listening-in to the qualitative and quantitative data collection processes
- Controlling for non-response bias
- Validating that interviews were conducted, through post-interview contact with respondents. Our experience is that 5–10% of the interviews should be validated.

6. Segmenting customers into groups requires sophisticated statistical procedures. My experience with statistical procedures suggests that cluster analysis and conjoint measurement methodology produce valid needs-based segmentation frameworks. It is important that these statistical tools be administered by a qualified research analyst.

CONCLUSION

The premise of this class note is that conducting needs-based segmentation studies represents a key leverage factor in developing and maintaining a sustainable competitive advantage. The note is designed to present detailed information on the needs-based segmentation process for consumer, service, and industrial markets. Hopefully, managers can gain confidence in the validity of the approach and champion conducting such studies in their organizations. Clear quantitative customer information regarding the road ahead can be a big competitive advantage. In the land of the blind, the one-eyed competitor has the advantage.

Appendix C

Terminology Used in This Book

THIS APPENDIX REVIEWS basic terminology presented in this book. While definitions are important, they are best understood when applied to real businesses situations.

WHAT IS A VISION STATEMENT?

A vision statement is a long-term perspective of what an organization is striving to become. Vision or Purpose answers the following question: What do we want to be? In his inaugural address, President John Kennedy presented a vision for the United States in the statement: "Move toward making the United States the greatest and most respected nation in the world."

WHAT IS A MISSION STATEMENT?

Successful organizations have clear mission statements with stated goals and time frames for reaching them. The mission or objective answers this question: "What will we accomplish?" President Kennedy supported his vision with the mission statement of "Put a human being on the moon by the end of the decade."

WHAT IS A VALUE STATEMENT?

The value statement defines the context and boundaries for decisions in implementing the vision and mission statements. Value statements answer these questions: "What do we believe in, and how will our beliefs impact choices?"

STATEMENT EXAMPLES

Following are some examples from leading businesses of the different statements defined above.

Volvo Corporation

Vision Statement: "To be the world's most desired and successful premium car brand."

Mission Statement: "To be number 5 in customer satisfaction (according to the J.D. Power Initial Quality Study) by 2000 and number 3 by 2003."

Value Statement: "Stop keeping secrets about customer complaints; give employees a system for open communication and a broad view of the customer value-added process that encompasses the vehicle sales and service experience throughout the life of the vehicle."

Fabri-Kal Corporation

Vision Statement: "Be a world-class manufacturer of quality plastic parts and packages."

Mission Statement: "Achieve total customer satisfaction; be a growing and financially sound company, providing a fair return to shareholders."

Value Statement: "Manage operations and create products in an environmentally responsible manner."

WHAT IS STRATEGY?

Dictionaries define **strategy** as the science and art of military command as applied to the overall planning and conduct of large-scale combat operations. Strategy is compared to **tactics**, which dictionaries define as a plan of action resulting from the practice of this science. Strategy is a plan of action carried out tactically. Strategy answers this question: How will we get there?

The meaning of the word strategy comes from its use in a military context. Strategy was the plan for the deployment and use of military forces and material over a certain terrain to achieve a certain mission or objective. This plan was based on intelligence gathered regarding the opportunities or threats presented by the physical characteristics of the battlefield and those resulting from friendly or hostile residents. In addition, the strengths and weaknesses of the enemy forces relative to the resources available to the commander must be determined. An additional element was the timing of actions. Quick actions or surprise were considered an advantage that could alter the balance of forces.

The concept of strategy just discussed has been expanded to encompass areas such as politics, business, courtship, and the like. The analogy for business strategy is that the terrain is the broad political, economic, social, and technological environment. The enemy is the competition, and the resources to confront the enemy are composed of the people and assets possessed by the firm. In this context, business strategy can be thought of as the act of making choices that competitors fail to consider or prefer not to choose. The comprehensive business strategy is composed of components such as marketing strategy, financial strategy, manufacturing strategy, R&D strategy, and human resource strategy.

The growth in worldwide competition and changes in information technology have increased customers' choices in the marketplace as well as the availability of market information for customers. These trends have dramatically changed the importance of marketing strategy in recent years. At the heart of any business strategy is a marketing strategy. Businesses exist to deliver products and services to markets. To the extent that businesses serve this purpose well and efficiently, they can grow and profit. By the same token, a firm's marketing strategy must be consistent with its overall business strategy.

From the manager's perspective, strategy is involved when a choice is made that is different from that of a competitor. Copying the actions of a competitor is not strategy. There is no differential advantage in copying a competitor. All strategies are controversial because good arguments can be made for other choices. Consequently, the wise manager chooses to support strategic choices with fact-based information, such as a needs-based segmentation study.

Strategic choice implies trade-offs about resource allocation. Strategy is both about today and the future. Strategy is about uncertainty since it is about making choices today that impact future performance. Consequently, forecasting is an inherent component of strategic choices. The monitoring of market structures using needs-based segmentation studies should provide important facts to facilitate the forecasting process.

WHAT IS MARKETING STRATEGY?

Marketing strategy is composed of four interdependent decisions. They are: (1) target market selection, (2) target competitor selection, (3) determining the value proposition, and (4) determining the aggressiveness of the marketing program.

1. Target Market Selection

The most critical of the four marketing strategy decisions is target market selection. Which markets will be served? What emphasis will be placed on these markets? The answers to these questions rest on a long-run analysis of the evolution of the markets and their requirements. The fundamental issue here pertains to future sources of revenue for the business. Consequently, marketing strategy deals with a long-range vision of future market opportunities. A critical component of this analysis is the segmentation of the market into homogeneous groupings of needs and buying processes. The forecasting of the nature and size of customer segments is a critical component of the marketing strategy.

2. Target Competitor Selection

This component requires a complete understanding of the competitors in the selected target market. The attractiveness of market opportunities is significantly impacted by the nature and degree of current and future competitive intensity. A comprehensive understanding of competitive objectives and capabilities is essential to the prediction of a firm's degree of success in the competition for revenue and profits. Just like in a poker game, it is very important that the organization clearly understand whom they are competing against.

3. Value Proposition

The value proposition identifies the key reason(s) that will motivate customers to purchase from your organization rather than from competitors. It refers to the positioning of the marketing program in the target consumer's mind relative to competitive products. This statement of how the organization proposes to deliver superior value to customers should be the firm's single most important organizing principle. It must be based on organizational skills and resources that deliver value as perceived by the customer.

Business professor Robert S. Kaplan and business executive David P. Norton report in their book *Putting the Balanced Scorecard to Work*: "In our research, we have found that although a clear definition of the value proposition is the single most important step in developing a strategy, approximately three-quarters of executive teams do not have consensus about this basic information."[1]

It is important to remember that value is defined in the marketplace. In the factory, we add costs. Value is created when the customer pays the organization more for the product or service than the total costs incurred to create and deliver the product/service to the marketplace. Revenue and profit are measures of the value created. It is the reward for creating a satisfied customer.

4. Aggressiveness

The effectiveness of a marketing program is dependent on the size of the monetary muscle used to implement the marketing mix. It is important to recognize that aggressiveness is not related to the absolute monetary budget but rather the relative budget compared to competitors. To be heard in a crowded room requires speaking louder than the competition.

The ability to achieve the best marketing mix is fundamental to creating value and will depend on a thorough analysis of the particular marketing situation, the creativity of the individuals planning the marketing program, and the attention to detail in the execution. The multitude of decisions and the nature of coordination required for delivery of effective marketing strategies to the marketplace make marketing a crucial, challenging, and demanding element in a firm's business strategy.

WHAT IS STRATEGIC MARKETING PLANNING?

The organizational process that supports the development of a marketing strategy is called the strategic marketing planning process. Dwight Eisenhower is quoted as stating, "Plans are nothing, and Planning is everything."

1. Situational Analysis

The planning process starts with a situational analysis. The purpose of the situational analysis is to present management with a systematic record of the strategic issues driving their business. This involves analyzing four areas: (1) industry, (2) competition, (3) markets, and (4) customers. Strategic issues are summarized in a SWOT analysis (Strengths, Weaknesses, Opportunities, and Threats). This historical analysis of critical issues forms the backdrop for forecasting possible future environmental scenarios. These scenarios form the key planning assumptions for the rest of the planning process.

2. Setting Objectives

The second component of the strategic marketing planning process involves setting objectives. It is important to define objectives in a balanced framework of financial, customer, internal, and innovation measures.

3. Strategic Options

The third component of the process is to select strategic options to accomplish these objectives. Strategic options can be framed as resource allocation decisions regarding new products and/or existing products in new markets and/or existing markets.

4. Marketing Strategy Statement

The fourth component involves development of a marketing strategy statement. As discussed previously, this statement reflects strategic choices as to (1) target markets, (2) target competitors, (3) value proposition, and (4) aggressiveness.

5. Marketing Program or Marketing Mix

The fifth component involves the multitude of decisions regarding the tactical aspects of the marketing program. The term "marketing mix" refers to decisions by the organization regarding the four Ps: (1) product/service policy, (2) placement or distribution policy, (3) promotion policy, and (4) price policy. Management has many choices in each of the four components of the marketing program.

6. Budget and Supporting Documents

The final component of the strategic marketing planning process is the development of a budget and of supporting documents to measure and control the marketing strategy.

Acknowledgments

A S MENTIONED IN its preface, this book is the result of requests from students and business executives to have a document that summarizes the material I presented in MBA classes and executive education programs over the years. Special thanks go to Professor Aneel Karnari, whom I have taught with around the world in these educational programs. Much of the material presented in the book reflects my interactions with him during our development of innovative course material for the Strategic Marketing classes we taught together.

I am equally indebted to Edwin Amonsen, President of Michigan Marketing Associates, who was an innovator in the implementation of needs-based segmentation. Ed's skills in designing and analyzing research data provided me with insights into the potential of needs-based segmentation in the foundation of strategic marketing and competitive analysis.

The format of this book required several revisions. Professor Priscilla Rogers read the original version and made many helpful suggestions, for which I thank her. Special thanks go to Janet Cannon, my editor. While Janet's background is not in business, she quickly grasped the strategic concepts presented and suggested major changes in how to reposition this book's material in a readable format. My thanks also to Mark Bialek for the Chapter 1 photo of the Ross School of Business.

Finally, I would like to thank my wife Linda, who put up with yet another writing project.

About the Author

JAMES R. TAYLOR, Ph.D. is Professor Emeritus of Marketing as well as previous holder of the S.S. Kresge Chair at the Ross School of Business, University of Michigan. He received his Ph.D. from the University of Minnesota with a specialization in marketing, psychology, and statistics. His dissertation "An Empirical Evaluation of Coombs's Unfolding Theory" won the American Marketing Association Dissertation Award. Dr. Taylor's teaching and research interests are in the areas of strategic marketing planning, market segmentation, marketing research, and marketing management. During his academic career, he has been area chair for marketing, the chair of fifteen Ph.D. dissertations, and a member of sixteen additional dissertations.

Dr. Taylor has published over forty articles in academic journals, including in *The Journal of Marketing*, *Journal of Marketing Research*, and *Journal of Consumer Research*. He has authored ten books and monographs, including *Modern Marketing Research, Concepts, Methods, and Cases* (Thomson Learning, 2008), *Emerging Markets Simulation* (Interpretive Simulations, 2006), *Marketing Research: An Applied Approach and Exercises in Marketing Research, 5th edition* (New York: McGraw-Hill, 1995), and *Introduction to Marketing Management, Text, and Cases, 5th edition* (Chicago, Irwin, 1985).

Professional activity for Dr. Taylor includes membership in the American Marketing Association and Association for Consumer Research. He has been Vice President of the Detroit Chapter of the American Marketing Association, Executive Secretary of the Association of Consumer Research, and on the Editorial Board of *The Journal of Marketing*, *Journal of Marketing Research*, and *The Journal of Consumer Research*.

Dr. Taylor's business experience includes seven years with General Mills, Inc., in marketing and new product development. In addition, he has been a project director for Accenture Consulting and Booz Allen Hamilton. Over his career, Dr. Taylor has served as a consultant to numerous business organizations such as General Electric, Ford, DuPont, G.T.E., Johnson & Johnson, General Foods, and Procter & Gamble. He actively participates in company management education programs and has lectured in Brazil, Singapore, Hungary, France, Taiwan, Poland, Russia, Malaysia, Switzerland, and the United Kingdom.

Notes

Chapter 1. Strategic Marketing Class

1. Southwest case study 9-575-061 (A) (B), 9-694-023, Harvard Business School.

2. Ibid.

3. Ross Business School case study based on student project in India.

Chapter 2. Summer Consulting Adventure

1. Ross School of Business case study and presentation by company executives.

Chapter 3. Market Research Procedures Class

1. "Examples of Segmentation Strategies in Consumer Markets." Graduate Research Paper, Winter Term 1992, Ross School of Business.

Chapter 4. MBA Field Project

1. Kaplan, Robert S., and David P. Norton. "Having Trouble with Your Strategy? Then Map It." Harvard Business Review, September 1, 2000.

2. *How Can We Help You?* Videotape, supplied by Mobil Corp.

Chapter 5. Case Study Research Project

1. Material for this chapter was adapted from Harvard Business School case studies 9-596-058, 9-799-158, 9-598-116, and 9-300-060 (Boston: Harvard Business School Publishing).

2. MacIntyre, John. *Fact of Life: Computers.* New York: McGraw-Hill, Inc., 1997.

3. Open architecture refers to a computer system in which all the system specifications are made public so that other companies can be encouraged to develop add-on products such as peripherals and other extensions for the system.

4. Research grant from the Hewlett Packard Corporation to Professor Taylor, The University of Michigan.

5. Steffens, John. *Computer Industry Forecasts and New Games: Strategic Competition in the PC Revolution.* New York: Pergamum Press, 1994.

Appendix A. Class Note

1. Kaplan, Robert S., and David P. Norton. "Having Trouble with Your Strategy? Then Map It." Harvard Business Review, September 1, 2000.

2. Lutz, Bob. "Life Lessons from the Car Guy." The Wall Street Journal, June 11, 2011.

Appendix C. Terminology Used in This Book

1. Kaplan, Robert S., and David P. Norton. "Having Trouble with Your Strategy? Then Map It." Harvard Business Review, September 1, 2000.

Lightning Source UK Ltd.
Milton Keynes UK
UKHW020621310822
408078UK00008B/1832

Wouldn't it be great if you had a tool for accurately predicting businesses' future successes or failures and winners or losers based on something other than historical facts and figures about those businesses? . . .

Written by a leading business school professor, this book presents business executives, investors, students, educators, and others with that tool! "Market Segmentation" is the division of businesses' potential customers into groups based on a wide range of characteristics, including demographics, income and education levels, interests, and more. And "Needs-Based Market Segmentation," as presented in this book, is an innovative form of market segmentation that allows accurate forecasts of businesses' future competitive performance (successes and failures, winners and losers) by measuring today's consumer and business needs.

This book is the result of requests from students and business executives to have a document that summarizes material the author, Professor James R. Taylor, presented in MBA classes and executive education programs during his over forty-year teaching and research career at the University of Michigan's famed Ross School of Business. The book is cleverly written as a recounting of the real-life progression of a business school student named Bob as he learned about the Needs-Based Market Segmentation process in school and then used that process to make millions in the stock market and retire early. Are you the next Bob? Read and find out.

JAMES R. TAYLOR, Ph.D. is Professor Emeritus of Marketing and a previous holder of the S.S. Kresge Chair at the Ross School of Business, University of Michigan. He received his Ph.D. from the University of Minnesota, specializing in marketing, psychology, and statistics. Dr. Taylor's teaching and research interests include strategic marketing planning, market segmentation, marketing research, and marketing management. During his academic career, he has been area chair for marketing and the chair of fifteen Ph.D. dissertations. Dr. Taylor has published over forty articles in academic journals, and he has authored ten books and monographs. He has had years of business experience in marketing and new product development, as a project director, and as a consultant to numerous businesses. Dr. Taylor actively participates in company management education programs and has lectured around the world.

Van Rye
PUBLISHING
www.vanryepublishing.com